WORKING WITH THE WOOL

How to Weave a Navajo Rug

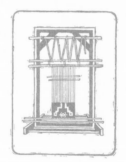

WORKING WITH THE WOOL

BY NOËL BENNETT AND TIANA BIGHORSE

With drawings by Robert Jacobson

NORTHLAND PRESS / FLAGSTAFF

Seventh Printing — December 1977

ISBN 0–87358–084–2
Library of Congress Catalog Number 73–174994

NORTHLAND PRESS / FLAGSTAFF, ARIZONA 86001

Contents

Photograph by Peter Bloomer

About the Authors

TIANA BIGHORSE was born north of Tuba City, Arizona in 1917 to the Bitterwater clan. At the age of seven she began two important aspects of her life: she started school (Tuba City Boarding School) and she started to weave. Whereas her school career lasted through the ninth grade (a remarkable achievement for a Navajo of her generation), her weaving career has lasted even longer, soon half a century.

It was her mother who taught her the weaving skill, just as she had been taught by her mother before her. Tiana's mother wove large rugs and was very mindful of their quality. She passed on this pride to her daughter.

Although Tiana's married name is Butler, she has chosen to use Bighorse for this book, in honor of her father, "a brave and courageous man, who defended the Navajo land against Spaniards, Mexicans, and the cavalry." Her father, so named for the size of his horses, lived a strong life until he died at the age of ninety-two.

"He always liked his name, Bighorse."

Tiana Bighorse Butler has lived her life on the western side of the reservation in the Tuba City area.

NOËL KIRKISH BENNETT was born in California in 1939. A *cum laude* graduate of Stanford University (B.A. 1961, Art with Honors in Humanities; M.A. 1962, Education), she taught at the College of Notre Dame. Her interest in Navajo weaving grew out of a background in art generally, and weaving specifically.

Noël's way of life on the Navajo reservation began in 1968 when her physician-husband joined the Public Health Service. In Tuba City,

Arizona she studied weaving under the expert tutelage of competent weavers such as Tiana Bighorse Butler and Helen Nonabah Tsinnie, learning the whole spectrum of the craft — from shearing the sheep, plant-dyeing the wool, carding and spinning, to the actual weaving.

After two years in Tuba City, she moved to Shonto, about an hour further into the hinterlands, where her husband began setting up a full-time medical station for Navajos living in this remote area. In Shonto, her understanding of weaving deepened, as she was able to compare notes with several of the prominent weavers of the area.

At present Noël Bennett lives in Corrales, New Mexico, near Albuquerque. She continues her work in Navajo weaving: writing, weaving, conducting workshops, and giving lectures and demonstrations. She is the author of *The Weaver's Pathway: A Clarification of the "Spirit Trail" in Navajo Weaving,* another Northland Press publication, which delves into Navajo spiritual beliefs connected with the weaver's art.

Preface

BECAUSE WE SEE the beauty of the Navajo loom, and feel you will, too, we are presenting a kind of manual: a means by which you may apprentice yourself to a Navajo weaver and partake of the satisfaction that comes from working with the wool.

When one approaches a Navajo hogan looking for someone special, the manner most effective is to inquire of the first young head appearing shyly from any doorway.

"Where's Grandmother?"

For oneself to set about looking for grandmother is futile. Hardworking head of the household, she may be out herding sheep; she may be in cooking supper; she may be over gathering dye plants.

"Nimásánísha? Where's Grandmother?"

And likely as not, the response accompanied by a pointing of the lips will be,

"N'leidi."

"Over there."

"She's working with the wool."

Working With the Wool was selected as the title of this book for it speaks of an interaction between the weaver and her medium, a oneness between the two, a kind of mutual understanding which has grown from long hours of association over many years.

Working With the Wool is essentially a resource book on the Navajo approach to weaving, and is intended for a wide variety of users:

It is written for people who are intrigued with the simplicity and directness of the Navajo weaving way, and yearn to give it a try.

It is for the free spirits who are drawn by a craft which involves little or no bought materials to begin, a craft in which the loom and tools can be fashioned from trees, and these when combined with a little know-how and a gift from a sheep, can produce an item both beautiful and functional.

It is for advanced weavers who are tired of the same techniques, who would like to learn from the ancients and incorporate new spirit into their already accomplished approach.

It is for artists in any medium who like the bold Navajo designs and have wished for a repository in which many have been collected.

Finally, it is for collectors who have long admired the products of the Navajo loom and often wondered about the process that gave them birth.

People who came to visit us on the reservation were enchanted by the beauty of the Navajo weaving process and product. Many wished that they, too, might become involved in the craft. But how would they learn? Just as it was impossible to find a Navajo weaver to teach each interested visitor, so was it equally impossible to take each one on personally.

In addition, school administrators, responding to needs of their students, were requesting help in formulating and developing a Navajo weaving program in their reservation boarding and public school curricula. It became clear that there was a need for this process to be interpreted and recorded so its availability could be expanded.

It was to fill these expressed needs that this publication was written. The purpose was not to present a lengthy discussion on the various types of Navajo designs in existence. It was not intended to be a scholarly research into Navajo weaving history. Nor was it to be a presentation of all the cultural beliefs that accompany the weaving process. Instead, *Working With the Wool* was meant to be a first step in making the Navajo weaving technique generally available to any interested person.

The joint authorship is one of the unique aspects of the book. With the exception of *Navajo Native Dyes* by Bryan and Young, no other of the more than fifty publications on Navajo weaving has had so much involvement on the part of the Navajo weaver.

One of the reasons why Tiana Bighorse has been interested in developing this manual is because she is concerned with the gradual disappearance of this skill among the younger Navajo girls. Perhaps this waning is inevitable. As with any culture in transition, traditional crafts are very often denigrated only to undergo a renaissance after the culture is once again integrated. Tiana, however, has hopes that this need not necessarily be the case; that with some foresight, this customary process could be averted. She has indicated that because the emerging Anglo life style is so different from the traditional way, it is very difficult for the Navajo girls to learn the weaving processes, which are no longer part of their everyday experiences. Faced with these realities, she would like this book to provide a method for Navajo girls to reclaim this art within the context of the new societal demands.

Another strong consideration for her participation is the natural desire to share her activity with others who are interested, no matter what their cultural background.

For these reasons, her involvement has been in a very real and very concerned way.

Introduction

NAVAJO WEAVING is an organic craft. The tools are basic, the process rhythmic, and the whole weaver-loom relationship a very natural one. Do not be surprised then, when the type of satisfaction you derive as you build your pattern is equally direct, basic and rhythmic. Do not be surprised when you find the workings of the loom to be so humble that you hear yourself whispering to no one in particular, "Now why didn't I ever think of that."

Remember as you manually tighten your warp and pack your weft, that this simplicity is the very reason the Navajo loom has persisted. Although the white man has attempted to introduce the Navajo to a "liberating, modern, faster" loom, his efforts have thus far had no effect.

Any Navajo knows that sheep demand pasture, and pastures need a rest. And whereas the heat of the summer is escaped in the heights, the cold of the winter is lessened in the valleys. Thus, it is natural that a semi-nomadic sheep raising people would recognize the beauty of a simple, portable loom — one that could be fashioned from materials at hand — and taken apart, rolled up and moved at any stage of the weaving process. Such beauty is self-evident.

Our feeling that this beauty is worth recording, preserving and sharing has provided the motivation for this book. We hope it will enrich your experience as it has ours.

The glossary of terms at the back of the book may be useful to you as you journey into this adventure.

Getting Started

3

BEFORE YOU BECOME INVOLVED with the equipment and technicalities of the process, we suggest you think ahead to your project and what kind of weaving a beginner might reasonably expect to complete. Also the size of your project will determine the type of equipment you will need. Until you become familiar with the new style of weaving, it is better to think small. Perhaps 10″ x 23″ would be an appropriate beginning. The diagram for a larger rug, shown on page 99, is a project you might undertake later.

A 10″ x 23″ weaving is useable in many ways. It is a good dresser size, looks well under a table arrangement, or can be doubled to make a purse or pouch for your weaving tools, knitting paraphernalia, etc. Students will undoubtedly appreciate it as a book bag; it easily accommodates a binder. Parents will find it a handy diaper bag. People who depend on the curative properties of herbs may carry it as a "medicine bag." Smoke-pouch and saddlebags are other possibilities.

If so doubled for a bag, this makes a receptacle about 10″ wide and 11½″ deep, a proportion which holds things securely. It can be handsomely secured at the top by a Navajo button and loop, or lined with cotton and zippered. More and more Navajo weavers are making purses, finding that this type of bag looks, lasts and wears extremely well. A shoulder strap is usually woven or braided and attached to provide a functional handle.

There is one consideration which may help you in your success.

It involves keeping a rough deadline in mind, so that your momentum is not allowed to wane, and your weaving will reach completion. You might plan on about two weeks for finishing the suggested 10″ x 23″ size, more or less, depending on how much time you give to it. An accomplished weaver such as Tiana Bighorse can complete it in one day.

Equipment

You will need to collect some essential equipment before starting to weave. We feel that making the loom and tools is a satisfying part of the process. However, if you would prefer purchasing these, Living Designs in Sunnyvale, California carries sturdy looms made according to directions contained herein. The Yarn Depot in San Francisco carries frames of two sizes, and still another type can be ordered from The Pendleton Shop in Sedona, Arizona. Since the nature of Navajo weaving requires that the loom be made of heavy material and mounted on a sturdy base, it is the considered opinion of the authors that the loom made at Living Designs is ideally suited and is shipped ready for use. Each of the other types mentioned here needs to be modified according to directions included in the Appendix.

Tools are similarly available. Refer to the chapter on *Supply Sources* near the end of the book for detailed information and addresses.

For weavers who are interested in fashioning their own loom and tools, directions follow.

THE LOOM

Navajo weaving is performed on a vertical loom. The weaver sits at the base on a pile of soft sheepskins. The tapestry of bright colors and intricate patterns rises before her.

You will find watching your weaving grow before you a unique experience. As you become more and more comfortable with the weaving process itself, you will be able to shift your attention away from the technical aspects toward the rhythm of the weave and the glory of being encompassed by design. In addition, if you choose to sit on progressively higher seats as the weaving develops, you will be able to see your composition as a whole, instead of weaving a few inches and then rolling it from view, as is necessary in the Anglo weaving tradition.

The loom should be larger than the weaving, allowing a foot clearance in length and width (six inches per side and one foot at the top). In instances in which the length of your weaving exceeds the height of your loom, see the Appendix for appropriate mounting of warp. The width of the weaving, however, should always be less than the width of your loom.

Many Navajo weavers anchor whatever rigid frame is available (a metal bed frame, for example) to their hogan for a loom. Some find a pair of trees outside which naturally grow the proper distance apart, and use them as uprights. Such approaches are not applicable to the conventional environment of a house and small yard. For these reasons directions will be given for constructing a free-standing loom.

One of the beautiful features of the Navajo loom is that it can cost you nothing to make if you are a scavenger, or it can be built of beautiful hardwood and incorporated into your decor as a refined piece of furniture.

Some of the non-Indian women who have undertaken weaving on the reservation have decided in favor of a large loom, which allows them to increase the size of subsequent weavings without building a new loom. A floor loom about three and a half by five and a half feet may dwarf the first small projects, but sets you up well for the next weaving which can be a substantial size floor rug (three by five feet) if you have the ambition. A double saddle blanket (thirty by sixty inches) can also be handled.

Most beginners, however, prefer a smaller loom (three by four feet). It is easier for a non-carpenter to construct and has the added advantage of portability (it can be hauled in an average car trunk). Additionally, people with back ailments can place it on a table and enjoy the comfort of weaving seated in a chair.

Although the loom described here may be constructed in any size, the measurements given are for the three by four foot size which is suitable for the suggested 10″ x 23″ weaving. Later it can accommodate the larger advanced project presented at the end of the book.

List of Supplies Needed for Construction of Loom

4 pcs.   TWO-BY-FOURs 34″ long (straight) for the crosspieces

2 pcs.   TWO-BY-FOURs 42″ long (straight) for the verticals

2 pcs.   TWO-BY-FOURs 30″ long (straight) for the legs

5   1″ DOWELS   36″ long (straight) for the beams
> Three of these dowels are not part of the constructed loom but are needed once warping begins. For the basic two dowels which will be used as upper and lower beams (see illustration), ¾″ metal pipe could be substituted.

6

4   FLAT CORNER IRONS 3½″ x ⅝″

16   FLAT HEAD WOOD SCREWS for above ¾″ #6

4   MACHINE BOLTS ⁵⁄₁₆″ x 3½ to attach upright frame to base

8   WASHERS for above

¼ lb.   BOX NAILS #10

2   ¼″ DOWELS 22″ long to be used as shed rods
> These are not part of the constructed loom, but are required for the warped loom. Willow sticks are traditional and preferable, if available.

1 pr.   LEATHER BOOT LACES 54″ long to bind top beam to uprights
> The leather look is usually the most aesthetically pleasing. However, rope, wire or 2 pipe straps may be used with equal success.

1 sheet   ROUGH SANDPAPER

2   ¾″ TWO-HOLE PIPE STRAPS to attach lower beam to legs, and necessary screws

Tools Needed

Hammer	Adjustable wrench	⁵⁄₁₆″ bit, optional
Screwdriver	Pliers	

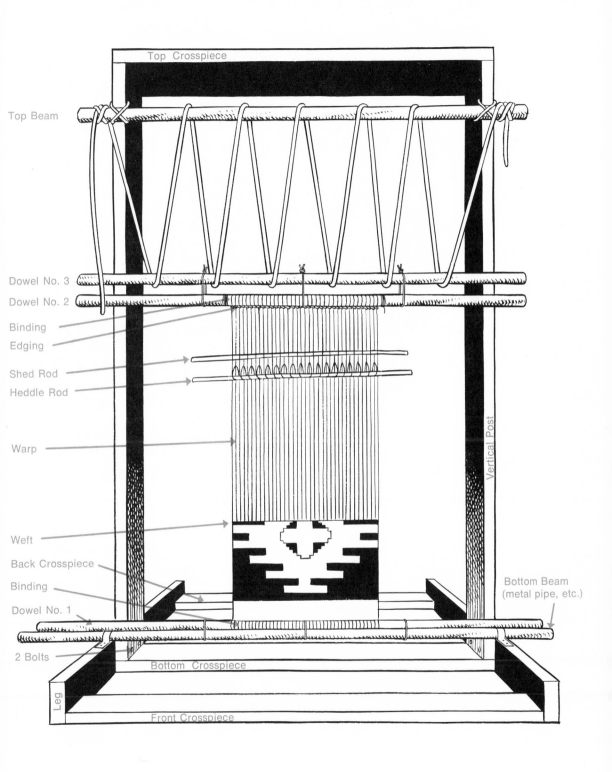

Top Crosspiece

Top Beam

Dowel No. 3

Dowel No. 2

Binding

Edging

Shed Rod

Heddle Rod

Warp

Weft

Back Crosspiece

Binding

Dowel No. 1

2 Bolts

Bottom Crosspiece

Leg

Front Crosspiece

Vertical Post

Bottom Beam
(metal pipe, etc.)

Design and Construction of Loom

This loom has been designed for the following features:

1. The weaver needs free and wide access to the loom. To achieve this the legs are placed at outer edges of loom and forward bracing of vertical posts is not used. Such bracing would interfere with insertion of batten.

2. The loom needs to be solidly built so no extraneous side motion occurs. Bracing to this effect is achieved by application of flat corner irons screwed to rear of loom frame.

3. The loom must be built of heavy construction to provide weight which counters the pull on shed rods. A front cross beam is provided upon which the weaver may lean with no discomfort, while her weight adds to loom stability. The connecting back crosspiece provides similar ballast while creating a place for additional weight if needed. (Weavers may place rocks, bricks, cinderblocks, etc., here.)

4. The weaving needs to be held in front of the loom proper so batten insertion will not be continually hindered by the vertical posts. The top and bottom beams are therefore designated to be longer than the loom width and thereby hold warp in desired forward position.

CONSTRUCTION PROCEDURE

1. Nail two 2″ x 4″ x 42″ pieces to two 2″ x 4″ x 34″ pieces to make a frame with dimensions 34″ x 46″.

2. Screw flat corner irons to rear of four corners.

3. Nail legs to front and back crosspieces.

4. Bolt upright frame to base: a. Drill two ⅜″ holes through bottom of frame and base on each side of loom. b. Insert a bolt with washer through each hole after drilling. c. When all four bolts are in place, add washer and nut to each. Tighten each with wrench and pliers.

5. Attach upper beam to top of vertical posts by chosen method: a. *With leather:* Drill hole in vertical posts and pass leather through hole and around top beam several times. b. *With pipe straps:* Attach top beam with two pipe straps screwed into position.

6. Attach lower beam to top of legs by screwing pipe straps into position.

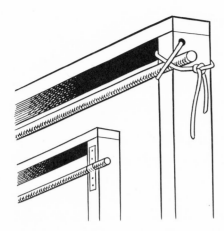

Figure 1: *Alternate methods of attaching upper beam to vertical post.*

Additional Loom Supplies

These items are not part of the loom proper, but are included in the loom supply list, as well as in the warping supply list. They are discussed here in detail in case you are scavenging your loom and need time to locate materials.

3 1″ DOWELS or BROOMSTICKS 36″ long (straight) to mount warp on loom (See Dowels Nos. 1, 2, and 3 on drawing of loom.)

Since the reservation doesn't support instant lumberyards, reservation weavers have learned to keep old handles from brooms, rakes, shovels, hoes, etc. These are invaluable and every weaving household has a supply. Especially favored are the broomsticks, but you can substitute regular 1″ doweling for this purpose. The broomsticks or dowels need to be as long as the loom is wide so they can hold the weaving in front of the loom proper.

2 ¼″ DOWELS or WILLOW STICKS 22″ long for the shed rods

You will need two sticks of smaller diameter to help you manipulate the warps during weaving. These are called the shed rods and traditionally are made of willow or hardwood. Willow is a strong and supple wood. A straight branch is cut, tied to a broom handle so it will dry straight, and then kept in reserve until needed. These branches are about ¼″ thick and at least 12″ longer than weaving width. A ¼″ dowel, obtainable from the lumberyard, is also workable, as is a curtain rod, or other suitable metal rod.

Figure 2: *Common "pant leg" tool case.*

TOOLS

A good tool is highly valued by Navajo weavers and receives special care. Some are extremely specialized. A weaver usually has favorite ones, whose weight and balance are a part of her. Replacements for these are hard to come by.

Sometimes men make tools and sell them to the trading post as a source of income. However, weavers who take pride in their weaving and derive pleasure from the weaving process, do not buy these trading post tools. They prefer to make their own, or have a member of their family make them under close supervision.

A few tools are inherited from mothers and grandmothers. These old wooden implements, shiny and smooth from long usage and loving care, are treasured accordingly.

Some weavers give expression to the power they feel in a tool. To lend a tool to someone is to give of your power. Thus, it is not frequent that a tool is lent or given unless, of course, it is to a close and trusted friend, and then it is not just the loan of a tool, but a gift of energy and ideas as well.

The Case

As you are gathering the equipment and tools for your loom, you will undoubtedly be looking for an orderly manner in which to keep them.

Figure 3: *Batten*   *Side View*   *Cross Section*

Top View

One common way among the Navajo weavers is to stitch a canvas case. Some weavers rip up an old pair of their husband's jeans, using one leg as a ready-made case. All that is required here is to stitch the bottom together and secure the top with a piece of leather or rope.

The Batten

The batten is one of the most cherished and basic weaving tools. It is used to separate warp sets so a weft may be passed. It is, of necessity, made of hardwood, for it has much interaction with the tight warp threads and will groove beyond usage if a softwood has been used. In addition, it must be capable of polishing to a highly refined finish, so as not to catch the warp threads.

Any hardwood may be used: oak, walnut, mahogany, reservation "cedar," etc. Oak is one of the favorites. It lasts a long time and takes on a beautiful patina from repeated contact with body oils and from constant rubbing of warp threads.

The purpose of this flat tool is to separate the warp strands sufficiently to allow passage of a weft through, hence the width of the batten. In addition, each is designed with a slight curve toward the front end, which aids in its insertion between warp threads.

For your first rather small project, we suggest two battens: one of medium width (1″) and one smaller (½″). The medium one will be used for the first half of the weaving, and the narrower one will be

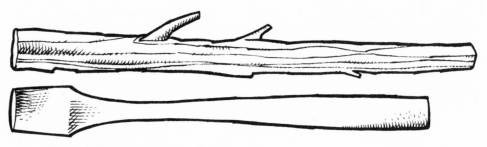

Figure 4: *Batten wood sources — hardwood branch and axe handle.*

12

substituted as the remaining weaving space gets smaller. When a few inches from completion, a refined ¼" dowel may be used, or an umbrella rib. These will be discussed later.

Because the batten is such a basic tool, we take time here to describe its ideal attributes and the way in which it can be fashioned. However, weavers who do not wish to put time in on this tool can consult the chapter on *Supply Sources.*

FOR THOSE WHO WANT TO MAKE THEIR BATTENS

On your wanderings through a forested area, keep a lookout for a branch of hardwood, which is about 1½" in diameter, and another about half that size. The branch you are looking for should have a section which is basically straight for about 27". After cutting it, remove the bark and flatten it on two sides (rasp, saw, sander) until it is about ⅜" thick. The sides to flatten are determined by the shape of the branch, and by which end has a slight curve. The top and bottom edges should be quite straight. The curve should be on the left and ease gently toward you.

When the front and back surfaces have been flattened, put the end with the curve to your left and round the lateral ends as shown in Figure 3. The top and bottom edges are slightly thinned — the bottom edge a little more so than the top. Sanding adds the final touch and the batten is now ready.

Figure 5: *One method for shaping batten.*

When a hardwood branch is not available for making the batten, an axe handle or broken baseball bat can be substituted. The axe handle is more adaptable due to the already flattened sides. A baseball bat may take power tools to transform it.

When a weaver has a batten which does not curve enough, one remedy is to warp it. This is done by coating it liberally with grease (shortening, etc.) and burying it in wet sand for a week. A heavy weight is placed at the point where the curve should be. Nature then joins in shaping the tool.

The Weaving Fork

The weaving fork is another of the cherished tools and is used to beat the weft into position. These, too, are made of hardwood from a found branch, or from a hammer or axe handle which weavers can salvage upon breakage.

The forks are not difficult to buy. Weaving stores generally have some type, as it is fairly standard equipment in many weaving methods. For Navajo forks, consult chapter on *Supply Sources.* For those in a hurry, a heavy table fork might be a temporary solution.

Although weavers have several forks among their weaving paraphernalia, one of the size and shape indicated here will suffice for this small project.

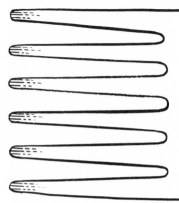

FOR THOSE WHO WANT TO MAKE THEIR FORKS

Obtain one piece of hard, heavy wood which measures at least ½" x 2" x 12". The basic shape is first drawn on the wood, and the piece then contoured accordingly by rasping, filing, and sanding.

The tines of the fork are made by sawing straight lines for about 2" every ¼". The points are then whittled and sanded to a taper, the final product being ½" in the middle and slightly thinner at the edges.

The area between the tines should be sufficiently wide so as not to bind the warp threads upon beating.

Other Tools

There are a few other items which you might be looking for. The first is a 5" curved sacking needle which is used at the end of the weaving when inserting the weft is difficult.

The other, also used at the end, is an old umbrella rib.

The rib, although of great help in the weaving, is not indispensable. It may be replaced by a very small ¼" batten. Since this is the same size as the shed rod dowels, we suggest that you treat the ends of one dowel as for a batten. This dowel may function as the top shed rod until about 3" from the top of the weaving, when the tightness will necessitate removal. It may then be used as the smallest batten.

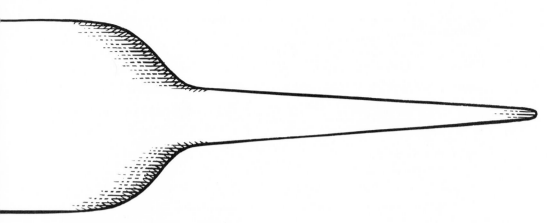

Figure 6: *Fork pattern, actual size.*

15

Figure 7: *Sacking needle, top and side views.*

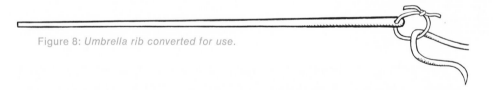

Figure 8: *Umbrella rib converted for use.*

Each Navajo weaver usually has an extensive set of tools. Although not required here, an average set might include:

Two forks: 1 large — 2″ wide   Battens: 1½″, 1″, ¾″, ½″, ¼″,
              1 small — 1″ wide   and smaller reeds.

Umbrella rib • Sacking needle • Shuttles: two or three straight
                          twigs of wood with broken ends (greasewood).

YARN

A Navajo rug is made up of three types of yarn:

1. The *Warp,* a thin, tightly spun yarn, is initially strung on the loom. It has inherent strength as it must be able to withstand great tension.

2. The *Weft,* a larger, fluffier yarn, is woven between the stretched warp so as to completely cover it in a tapestry weave. It is this yarn that is responsible for the beautiful texture of Navajo rugs.

3. The *Edging Cord,* a two-ply handspun yarn, is used on the ends and sides of the rug in the selvage position, to increase wearability.

All yarns contain much of the natural sheep oil, which largely accounts for the durability and resilience for which Navajo rugs are known. The lanolin content also provides some resistance to soiling.

Because each type of yarn is used in a special way, and because you may need to substitute commercial brands for these handspuns, each yarn type is taken up separately.

Warp

Navajo warp is difficult to secure. If you, yourself, spin, make a very tight thin yarn. The tightness must supply both strength and resistance to abrasion caused by fork. Treatment following spinning is described in the Appendix.

If you are not a spinner, substitute as follows:

WOOL

The best substitute for Navajo handspun is a strong, fine, tightly spun yarn available through the Yarn Depot and Living Designs.

A second recommendation is a four-ply mohair or camel hair which is available in a variety of natural colors. Its use requires the bowline knot. It may be ordered through the following stores:

Casa de las Tejedoras	Dharma Trading Co.
Creative Handweavers	The Weaving Depot
Handcraft House, Ltd.	The Yarn Depot

See chapter on *Supply Sources* for addresses.

A third recommendation is a Mexican handspun warp available through Casa de las Tejedoras. This yarn is strong, single-ply and similar to that of the Navajo.

Other suggestions include an 8/4 carpet warp. A respun worsted wool such as some Navajo weavers use is workable if a somewhat heavier warp is not objectionable.

COTTON

Some of the Navajo weavers use a cotton warp, at the expense of rug durability. In a wall hanging or purse, however, wear would not be an important consideration.

A second attribute of cotton warp is that when it is juxtaposed to smooth commercial weft, the combination is slippery, the packing is excessive and progress extremely slow. We suggest, therefore, that when cotton warp is used, it be combined with the rougher hand-spun weft.

Cotton carpet warp 8/4 in a natural color is available direct from Lily Mills Co. (Art. 414, 8 oz. tubes of 800 yards each.) Most yarn stores will have some in stock.

Weft

NAVAJO HANDSPUN

If you decide you would like to use Navajo handspun yarn, it can be purchased through specific weaving stores such as:

Custom Handweavers   The Weaving Depot
The Pendleton Shop

Other kinds of handspun may be substituted, and some from many countries are available at the above stores as well as through:

Casa de las Tejedoras   Paula Simmons
Creative Handweavers   Some Place
Handcraft House, Ltd.   The Yarn Depot
Dharma Trading Co.

See chapter on *Supply Sources* for addresses.

The main criteria in the selection of handspun yarns are not only the color relationships, but also the *uniformity of size and twist between colors.* Using large and small yarn, or tightly and loosely spun yarns in the same rug, causes rows to be uneven, stripes to wiggle across the rug, and the weaving line to have high and low areas which demand constant adjustment.

COMMERCIAL YARN

Another more readily available yarn is the commercially spun type. Some which are single ply have the quality of handspun. Most, however, cause a sacrifice in the lovely handspun texture of the final product.

One of the positive features of commercial yarn is that you are assured of all colors being the same weight, size, and twist. Commercial yarn is also less expensive.

Since so many kinds and weights are available, and the size affects the warp setting, this aspect will be treated more fully here. A detailed section on appropriate wefts and their sources follows.

WEFT: SIZES AND SOURCES

The weight and spin of the weft determines the warp setting. To help the beginner achieve a good ratio we have prepared a list with specific yarns and warp spacings that will work well together. In case the yarn you select is not on these lists, or your yarn is an in-between size, we recommend that you use the wider spacing of warps given in the first category.

Yarns with 400–700 yards/lb. generally do well with an
8-warp-per-inch setting (warp-turns ¼″ apart).

EXAMPLES	SOURCES
1. Navajo Handspun single-ply, medium weight	Living Designs The Pendleton Shop Custom Handweavers
2. Greek Yarn, medium weight single-ply, 500 yds./lb.	Living Designs Handcraft House, Ltd. Casa de las Tejedoras

3. Scandinavian Yarn single-ply, 650 yds./lb. fine but tightly spun	Living Designs The Yarn Depot Dharma Trading Co.
4. Ecuador Indian Handspun single-ply, 600 yds./lb. fibers straight and long	Dharma Trading Co.
5. Carpet Yarn three-ply, 480 yds./lb.	The Yarn Depot
6. English Yarn two-ply, 620 yds./lb.	Knit and Purl Yarn Shop Handcraft House, Ltd.

See chapter on *Supply Sources* for addresses.

*Yarns with 700–900 yards/lb. generally do well with a
12 warp-per-inch setting (warp turns ⅛″ apart).*

Fine yarns in this category are not recommended for a beginner, as using them considerably slows weaving — twice as many rows being needed to weave an inch.

EXAMPLES	SOURCES
1. Ecuador Indian Yarn single-ply, soft spun 800 yds./lb.	Dharma Trading Co.
2. Mexican Yarn, fine single-ply, soft spun 800 yds./lb.	The Yarn Depot Dharma Trading Co.
3. Greek Yarn, fine single-ply, 925 yds./lb.	Handcraft House, Ltd.
4. Carpet Yarn two-ply, 900 yds./lb.	The Yarn Depot

See chapter on *Supply Sources* for addresses.

WEFT: QUANTITIES NEEDED

The following chart can be used to approximate the amount of Navajo weft you will need for projects of varying sizes.

SIZE OF PROJECT	APPROX. AMOUNT WEFT NEEDED	EXAMPLES
225 square inches	½ lb.	10″ x 23″ (purse when doubled)
450 square inches	1 lb.	16″ x 28″ table mat
675 square inches	1½ lb.	19″ x 36″ double, makes 19 x 18 pillow
900 square inches	2 lb.	30″ x 30″ single saddle blanket
1125 square inches	2½ lb.	24″ x 46″ narrow wall hanging
1350 square inches	3 lb.	30″ x 46″ area rug
1575 square inches	3½ lb.	31″ x 50″ area rug
1800 square inches	4 lb.	30″ x 60″ double saddle blanket

The above estimates are based on rugs in which weft is firmly packed and warp is set ¼″ between each warp turn, or 8/inch. The square inches of a project can be determined by multiplying (in inches) the width of the project by its length.

Edging Cord

The edging cord is a two-ply yarn which *you will make from the regular weft.* The color is determined by the color of the weft at the bottom and top of your weaving. The two should match, or at least blend, unless decorative contrast is desired.

Following is a procedure for spinning edging cord from weft:

1. Needed for end edging cord: Two lengths of yarn measuring four times the weaving width, plus 50″ (90″ for the 10″ x 23″ project). Yellow is used here to coordinate with the first yellow stripe of the project. Treat each piece of weft separately and identically.

2. Double the yarn. Spin doubled yarn *tightly* on spindle or between palms in a direction opposite initial spin.

3. *Hold ends securely so spin is not released.*

4. Submerge in water until thoroughly wet.

5. *Tightly* stretch the over-spun yarn between two trees, around

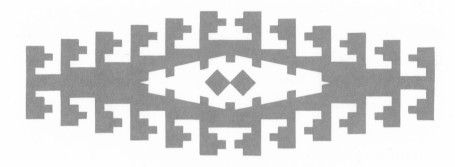

the back of a chair, or around a clothesline. Secure ends.

6. When yarn is dry, spin is set. Yarn may be removed, rolled into a ball, and set aside for usage.

Two end edging cords are needed for each weaving. For the 10″ x 23″ project, each should be at least 45″ finished length.

FOR SIDE EDGING CORDS

Additional side edging cords are optional (see page 41). If you are using them, you will need two which measure four times the *length* of the weaving plus 20 inches (finished two-ply size).

FOR BINDING

Some weavers use this same type of two-ply to bind the warp to the dowels during warping (see page 35). A heavy common twine such as Beacon Polished Parcel Post Twine will do the job equally well, and is recommended.

Warping the Loom

The foundation of weaving is warping the loom. It is this aspect which sets weaving in motion and starts ideas flowing. Some Navajo weavers, realizing the impetus from warping, give advice to the novice, saying: Never plan the design until you start to warp the loom.

And others, realizing that a warped loom is almost impossible to resist, say that as soon as you finish one weaving, start preparations for the next one. The loom must be warped again within four days, and thus, continued weaving is insured.

However, as exhilarating as it may be to warp and begin interacting with your creative project, a bit of reason and precision must temper the process. A certain amount of method and exactness is essential to the outcome of the weaving. It is much better to keep from making mistakes than to have to correct them, for sometimes they are never fully rectified.

It is for these reasons that a weaver is very particular when and where she warps her loom. She does not warp it when the hogan is filled with friends and relatives. She does not warp it when she has a few spare moments between herding the flock and making the dinner. No. She waits until she has a period of solitude. Children are asked to leave and she is alone.

The effect of the seclusion is twofold. She has the peace to concentrate on the process and on her forthcoming design, and she is assured that *nobody will bump her loom!*

Weavers who spiritually care about the process and products of weaving have certain taboos concerning the warping procedure. For instance, once begun, warping cannot be interrupted by eating, drinking, spitting, or sleeping. The process receives full attention.

Supplies Needed for Warping

Gather all supplies together before starting to warp.

The supplies listed here are based on the 10″ x 23″ project on a 3′ x 4′ loom. If a different weaving or loom size is chosen, check formula for figuring size and quantity of each material needed.

2 pcs.	TWO-BY-FOURs 3′ minimum length to be used in forming the temporary warping frame and should exceed the width of the weaving by 1′. They are reusable at each warping.
3 DOWELS	1″ (straight), or BROOMSTICKS, to be used to mount warp on loom. These should exceed width of loom.
4 NAILS	(sturdy)
1 HAMMER	
4 pcs.	ROPE or HEAVY TWINE (3′ if rope, 6′ if twine), used to tie broomstick dowels to two-by-fours to steady and secure warping frame
1 RULER	or measuring tape
1 PENCIL	
53 yds.	BALL OF WARP (see page 16) Estimate reached by multiplying width of weaving by number of individual warps per inch to determine total warp ends. This number is then multiplied by the length of the weaving to determine overall length of warp required, in inches. Divide by 36 to reduce to yards.
2 SHED RODS	22″ long and ¼″ in diameter. (See page 9.) Can be willow branches or ¼″ dowels. Should exceed weaving width by 1′.

2 TWINE short lengths	1′ lengths to tie shed rods together
2 EDGING CORDS	45″ minimum lengths, strong 2-ply yellow. These are made of weft spun together according to directions, page 20. Make your edging cords prior to warping, so they will be dry and ready when needed. Estimate: 4 times the weaving width, plus 50″ for tassels and twining.
2 TWINE long lengths	160″ minimum, to be used in binding edged warp to the two 1″ dowels. Estimate based on 4″ per warp pair. Beacon Polished Parcel Post Twine recommended.
1 HEDDLE STRING	160″ used for making heddles. Medium weight cotton string such as seine twine. Smooth and flexible unpolished cotton will suffice. Estimate based on 4″ per warp pair.
6 WIRE pcs.	15″ each, sturdy. If picture hanging wire is used, each piece should be 30″ and used doubled. Beacon Polished Parcel Post Twine can be substituted; it too must be doubled. Used in mounting warp to loom.
1 COTTON ROPE	⅜″ cotton rope requires 15′ length. If clothesline rope or weavers' harness cord is used, 30′ are needed so rope can be doubled. Do not use nylon or seisal.

24

Warping Outline

Each of the following steps is explained in detail on subsequent pages.

    I. Make a temporary warping frame.

    II. Wind warp onto the temporary frame in a figure eight to create two sheds.

    III. Preserve the sheds with the shed rods.

    IV. Space warp turns with edging cord.

    V. Bind edged warp to two dowels.

    VI. Mount warp on upright permanent loom.

    VII. Tighten warp.

    VIII. Position shed rods.

    IX. Install side selvage cords. This is optional.

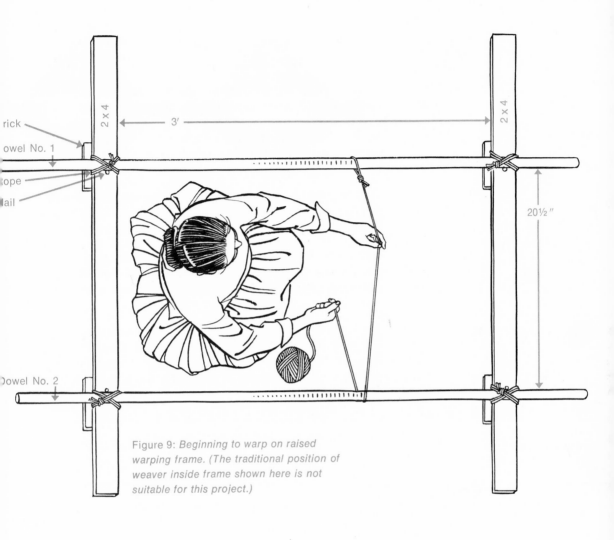

Brick
Dowel No. 1
Rope
Nail

2 x 4

3'

20½"

2 x 4

Dowel No. 2

Figure 9: *Beginning to warp on raised warping frame. (The traditional position of weaver inside frame shown here is not suitable for this project.)*

I. MAKE TEMPORARY WARPING FRAME

Materials Needed:

2 pcs. TWO-BY-FOURs 3′ long
2   1″ DOWELS or BROOMSTICKS
4   NAILS (sturdy)
1   HAMMER
4 pcs. ROPE or heavy twine, 3′ if rope, 6′ if twine

Refer to figure 9.

Read directions through before starting:

1. Place the two-by-fours on floor 30″ apart (any distance greater than width of weaving).

2. Hammer nails in each beam, 20½″ apart, leaving heads sticking out 1″. (Distance between nails, 2½″ less than desired length of completed weaving.)

3. Lay the two 1″ dowels across the two-by-four pieces on the outside of the nails.

4. Tie dowels in position with rope or heavy twine.

5. Raise frame from floor by setting corners on four equal-sized articles (bricks, blocks of wood, books, rocks, etc.). Clearance beneath frame should allow free rolling of warp. Check frame all sides to be sure corners are square.

6. Consider length of time available for following procedures. If

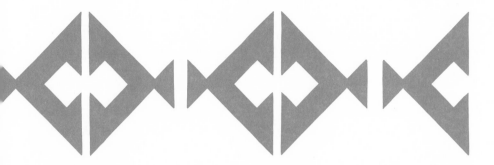

two hours are not available, postpone remaining steps until later. (A veteran weaver would require about one hour.)

II. WIND WARP ONTO THE TEMPORARY FRAME

Navajo warp is one continuous strand which is wound in a figure-eight pattern around two dowels. Although Navajo weavers use only the eye for spacing the warp, Anglo weavers who are just learning may find it useful to mark lines in the center of both dowels at ¼" intervals as follows:

For the 10" x 23" project:

1. Mark 41 lines for 10" in center of dowel No. 1. (on left).
2. Mark 40 lines for 9¾" in center of dowel No.2. (on right).

Note that directions herein will be for the ¼" spacing which will result in 8 warps per inch. If, from the section on *Weft Sizes* you have determined that your weft requires a different warp spacing, substitute your spacing in subsequent directions.

Materials Needed:

One temporary frame described on previous page.

One ball of warp, minimally 53 yards for the 10" x 23" project. (See section on *Warping Supplies* to determine yardage needed for projects of other dimensions.)

Procedure (read directions through before starting):

1. If there is sufficient room, sit inside the frame. If not, follow the

same procedure from outside, being careful not to bump the frame.

2. Tie one end of warp onto *far end* of dowel No. 1 (dowel on left). Use square knot. The knot should be 2″ from the dowel, and the loop should be on the first mark. If the knot slips, dab with glue.

3. Hold warp thread coming from dowel No. 1 in left hand. Hold ball of warp in right hand. Place warp ball over dowel No. 2 and roll it back toward you. Continue to hold warp string at constant tension with left hand.

4. Grasp warp strand near ball with right hand and pull until slack is taken up. Hold secure. Notice the tension you are applying and maintain this tension throughout the warping procedure. Although the amount of tension does not matter, being constant does! We suggest that the tension be snug but not binding.

5. Pick up ball of warp with left hand and place over dowel No. 1. Roll warp back toward you under dowel No. 1. With left hand pick up warp strand near the ball and pull until slack is taken up, freeing the right hand.

6. With free right hand adjust loops so they are ¼″ apart and each on a mark.

The warping pattern is essentially a figure eight around two dowels. The rhythm is: *Over and around under. Hold.*
Over and around under. Hold.
Establishing a rhythm helps keep tension constant.

As you continue the procedure remember:

- Always place warp *over* the dowel.
- Always return warp *under* the dowel.
- Always hold warp strand *under uniform tension.*
- *Do not bump the frame.*

7. Continue to place warp on alternate dowels at ¼″ intervals. Tie end of warp on same dowel as beginning was tied (dowel No. 1). Use a square knot to tie end 2″ from the dowel; cut off excess.

This makes an even number of warps which is preferable when rendering a symmetrical design. At four turns per inch there should be 40 "turns" counted on dowel No. 2, or 80 individual warps when counted in the center.

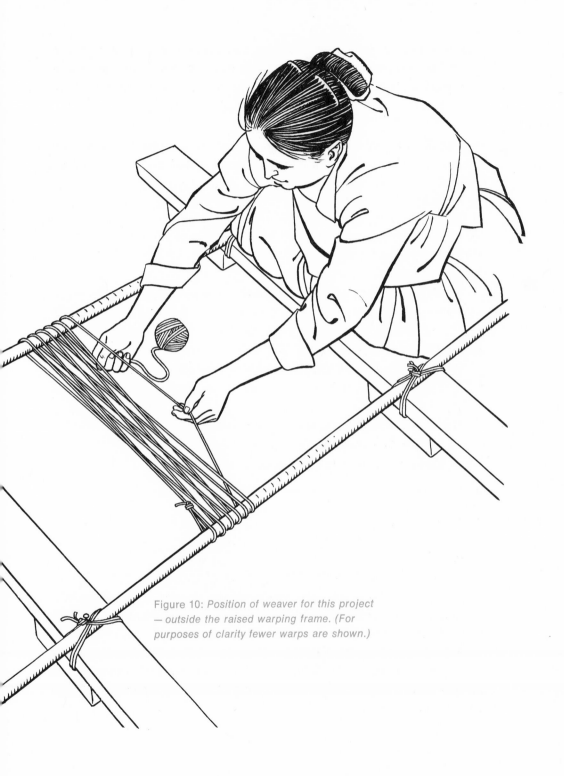

Figure 10: *Position of weaver for this project — outside the raised warping frame. (For purposes of clarity fewer warps are shown.)*

So as to promote communication, each time a warp is carried over the dowel and returned back under, it will henceforth be referred to as a *warp turn,* or *pair* of warp threads.

III. PRESERVE THE SHEDS

The figure eight which is established during the warping process is the first step in creating the two sheds which will help you manipulate your warps during weaving. This cross in the warp must be preserved as follows:

Materials Needed:

Two willow sticks for shed rods, or ¼" dowels.

Two 12" twine lengths.

Procedure:

1. Place a shed rod in each side of the figure eight, being careful of knotted warps on dowel No. 1 as follows: Standing behind dowel No. 1, insert rod from right to left under the knot of the first warp, through the subsequent loops, and over the knot on the last warp.

2. Slide these two rods *gently* toward the center crosses.

3. Tie the shed rods *snugly* together at each end with the 12" twine lengths.

If you are using one shed rod interchangeably with the smallest batten, place that shed rod in the half of the warp closest to dowel No. 2 (the one without knots).

IV. SPACE WARP TURNS WITH EDGING CORD

The Navajo weaver uses a heavy two-ply yarn to space the warps. By a process of twining this cord, permanent edging is formed which holds each pair of warps equidistant.

If you have used the marking method of equalizing the distances between warp turns, this procedure will serve only to stabilize their positions. The Navajo weaver, using just her eye to initially place the warp strands around the dowel, uses this procedure to equalize as well as to secure warp turns.

Although veteran weavers use no aids in spacing the warps, young Navajo girls just beginning in the method, are sometimes instructed to place a given object between warp pairs, and obtain a consistent

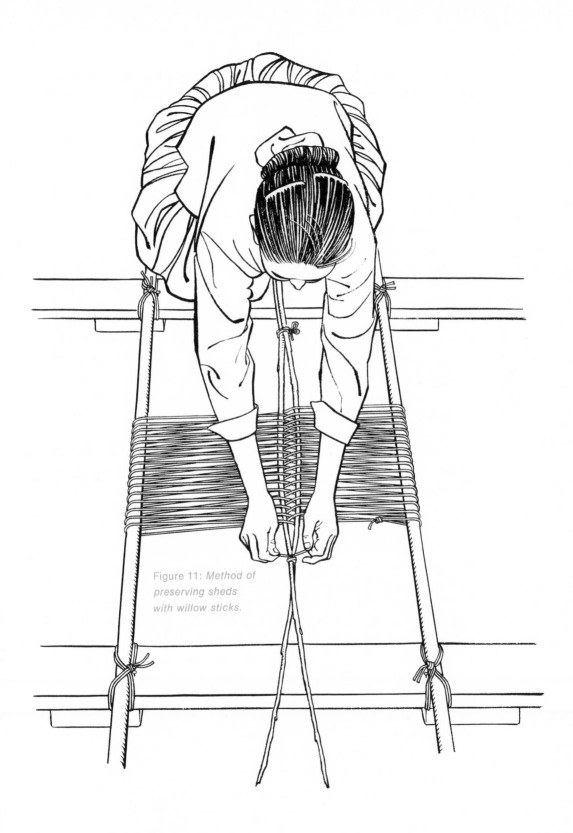

Figure 11: *Method of preserving sheds with willow sticks.*

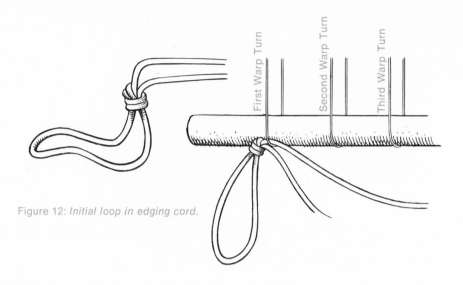

First Warp Turn

Second Warp Turn

Third Warp Turn

Figure 12: *Initial loop in edging cord.*

relationship in this manner. The size of the object used depends on the distance desired. The distance, in turn, is determined by the size yarn which is to be weft. (See chapter on *Yarn:* weft sizes).

Equivalent to placing warp turns on marks spaced at ⅛″ intervals, is inserting a large wooden matchstick between warps. Wire of an average coat hanger is also equivalent.

A thermometer, or other object with larger diameter, could be used to set the warps at 8 to the inch, or ¼″ between warp turns.

When the yarn is the very heavy handspun such as is often used for coarse saddle blankets, a pencil is sometimes the gauge.

As noted before, the color of your edging cord is determined by your design and color choice. If the first and last colors you will weave are dark, then a dark edging cord will be used. If the first wefts are white, then the cord will likewise correspond. Yellow is used here.

Because it is the twists which hold the warp turns the proper distances apart, for a relatively fine weave only one twist separates each turn. In heavier weaves two and occasionally three twists of the edging cord are needed to make larger spaces.

Materials Needed:

Two lengths of yellow edging cord 45″ long, previously prepared according to directions, page 20. Optional: One implement with diameter slightly under ¼″ (big nail, bolt, thermometer, etc.).

Procedure: Read directions through before starting.

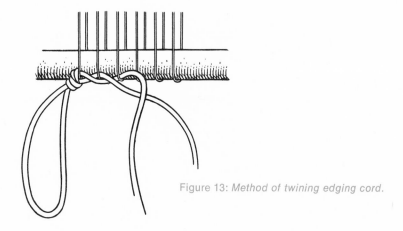

Figure 13: *Method of twining edging cord.*

1. Position yourself outside temporary frame behind dowel No. 1.

2. Double one 45″ length of yellow, two-ply edging cord. Tie a knot in the folded end, forming a 5″ loop.

3. Slip one end of the yellow edging cord through the first turn of the warp. Pull the end through until the edging-cord-knot is next to the warp turn. (At this point one end of the edging cord is beneath the first warp turn, the other is free. See figure 12.)

4. Hold the free end in your left hand, and the end coming from beneath the warp turn in your right hand. Exchange hands, placing the *right hand cord over the left.* A twist is thus formed in the edging cord following the first warp turn.

5. Slip the now right cord end (the one that was free) under the second warp turn. Once again, exchange hands, making sure *the cord coming from beneath the warp turn crosses on top.* The second warp turn is now stablilized. (See figure 13.)

    a. If you have marked the dowel, each warp turn should stay on the mark.

    b. If you have not marked the dowel, it is here you may insert the end of an implement between the first and second warp turns, thus spacing them ¼″ apart.

6. Continue this procedure, twisting the cord between each warp turn. The rhythm here is: *Under the warp and over the cord. Hold. Under the warp and over the cord. Hold.*

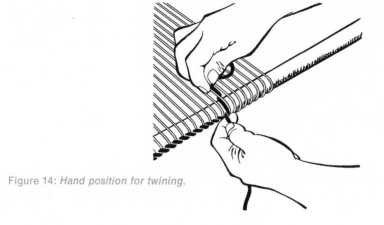

Figure 14: *Hand position for twining.*

When the right edge is reached, tie the ends of the edging cords together snugly, using the same knot as at the beginning.

7. Measure the entire width to be certain that it is 10″. Cut the excess 5″ past the knot.

8. The same procedure is repeated on the other dowel. When finished, once again measure to assure the 10″ width. If one side is longer than the other, simply slide the warp turns closer together or further apart, and re-tie the knot.

9. Check to be certain each individual warp turn has been bound.

Dismantle Temporary Frame

Now that the warp is spaced and edged, the temporary frame can be dismantled and the warp carefully removed.

1. Untie rope, binding corners of frame.
2. Lift dowels from behind nails.
3. Carefully slide dowels out of edged warp, keeping edging straight.
4. *Do not remove the tied shed rods.*

This part of warping is considered complete and you can now eat or sleep if desired. Otherwise, continue to the next section and the process that prepares the warp for being mounted onto the upright loom: binding the edged warp to the two dowels.

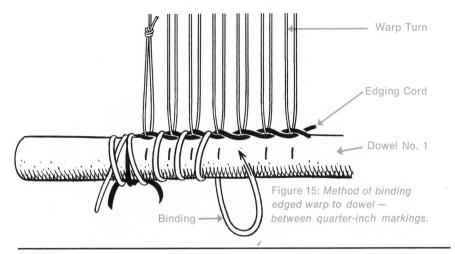

Warp Turn

Edging Cord

Dowel No. 1

Figure 15: *Method of binding edged warp to dowel — between quarter-inch markings.*

Binding

V. BIND EDGED WARP TO TWO DOWELS

Material Needed:

Two lengths of strong twine, each 160″.

Navajo weavers, preferring to spin their own binding, make a two-ply yarn which they are assured is strong enough to withstand the tremendous tension which the binding must bear. Since this binding is not part of the weaving, any strong twine such as Beacon Polished Parcel Post Twine is sufficient. Twine can be doubled if its strength is questionable.

Procedure: Read directions through before starting.

1. Lay edged warp on floor before you. Position yourself behind one edged end.

2. Center the dowel on the outside of the yellow edging, between you and the edging.

3. Start on the left side, cut the loop of yellow edging cord and tie the two ends *very tightly* around the dowel, to left of warp. Repeat on right side.

4. Use same treatment on opposite end of warp, with second dowel. Compare two dowels to be sure of identical 10″ widths.

5. (Many weavers like to rest the dowel on the warping frame for remaining steps.) Roll twine into ball that will pull out. Wrap twine securely around the tied yellow edging cord: three wraps. Wrap so

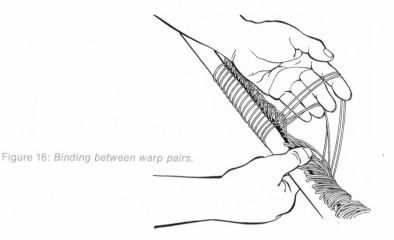

Figure 16: *Binding between warp pairs.*

the twine goes over the dowel and away, then returns under the dowel and toward you. Be certain that the wrapping is very tight and the edging cord ends well secured.

6. You will notice that the warp appears in pairs made by two sides of a warp turn. Continue the wrapping process, once around the dowel *between each of the warp turns,* thereby securing the yellow edging to the dowel. (The binding will go between marks.) Again the *tightness* of the wrap must be emphasized, as the tension upon this aspect is tremendous.

7. At the end of row, bind the yellow edging cord ends to the dowel securely with the twine, three wraps and tuck end under as before.

8. Repeat procedure on other end of the warp with the second dowel. Be certain to remeasure widths, and adjust if necessary.

VI. MOUNT WARP ON UPRIGHT LOOM

The warp is now suspended between two dowels and secured to each by means of strong twine. The next steps are very easy. You're now on the homestretch.

Materials Needed:

One dowel (No. 3)

Six 15″ pieces of wire or doubled heavy twine.

One rope: If heavy rope, 10′ will suffice. If clothesline or weavers' harness cord is used, 20′ is necessary; use doubled.

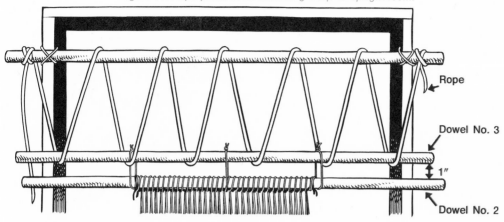

Rope

Dowel No. 3

1"

Dowel No. 2

37

Procedure: Read directions through before starting.

1. Tie dowel No. 2 to the new dowel (No. 3) in three places: At center and outside edges of weaving. Use pieces of wire or twine. Since dowels No. 2 and No. 3 should be a uniform 1" apart, some weavers place a 1" object between dowels as a temporary gauge to maintain uniformity. The center wire encircling dowel No. 2 should be placed beneath the edging cord. A nail may be used to force an opening to accommodate wire.

2. Center warp between vertical posts of loom and tie dowel No. 1 (the one on which the beginning and end of the warp was knotted) to the bottom beam (pipe) of the loom. Once again wire is used in three places. Here, however, the *dowel and pipe are flush.*

3. Attach one end of the long rope to the left side of the top beam just outside left edge of loom. Bind dowel No. 3 to top beam by encircling both from left to right (under and toward, over and away). When you reach the right side, secure the rope to the top beam by circling once or twice and tucking the end of the rope through the circle. (See figure 17.)

Untie Shed Rods

Until now the shed rods have been tied together to preserve the figure eight. These can now be untied: the top rod moved upward and the bottom one moved down.

Do not remove the shed rods.

If when the warp is mounted and tightened you find that the warp is longer on one side than the other, turn to the chapter on *Remedies* to ascertain the correction.

VII. TIGHTEN WARP

The tension on the warp is uniquely tight. It is this aspect of the Navajo weaving technique that allows the weft to be beaten down and woven so compactly. It is also this aspect (among others) which keeps your edges straight.

The tension can be compared to that on guitar strings: tight and resistant, but not rigid.

Cinching the warp is done from right to left as follows:

1. Reaching between top beam and dowel No. 3 with right hand push away the first section of rope crossing in back of the top beam. To its left is a continuation of that rope as it crosses in front of the top beam. Grasp this front rope in left hand and pull down steadily, taking up any slack which is created. The rhythm is that of cinching: while the left hand is steadily pulling downward, the right hand pushes, releases, pushes, releases.

2. Transfer the now tightened rope held by the left hand to your right hand. *Do not release the tension!* Your left hand is now free to grasp the next front section of rope and pull tightly to take up the slack. Hold firmly.

3. Release front rope in right hand, move left to adjacent back section and push this rope section away as before, once again creating slack which can be taken up with left hand.

4. This procedure of cinching and tightening the rope is continued right to left across the full width of the loom and secured at extreme left. Repeat full procedure across the loom several times until warp is very taut.

Enough tension is important. The following problems occurring during the weaving process indicate warp should be tighter:

1. Outside edges begin going in.
2. Outside edges begin going out.
3. Material begins to ripple.
4. Batten keeps turning flat instead of staying on edge.

Throughout first half of weaving, warp will need periodic tightening. Before a period of idleness (i.e., vacation) loosen warp.

VIII. POSITION SHED RODS

The basic weave in Navajo technique is the tapestry weave in which warp threads are completely covered up by the weft which travels alternately between warp strands.

1. Over . . . under . . . over . . . under . . . over . . .
2. Under . . . over . . . under . . . over . . . under . . .

The two devices employed to facilitate this threading are called *shed rods* and may be described as follows:

Upper Shed Rod: A stick situated behind alternate warps for the purpose of holding every other warp forward, and creating an opening for the passage of a weft.

Heddle Rod or *Lower Shed Rod:* A device for reversing the position of warps as described above. A stick is held horizontally in front of the warp, and string is looped from the rod to those warps in the back position. By pulling on this stick, the back warps may be brought into a forward position, creating an alternate opening for the passage of the next weft.

Positioning of the Shed Rods

The positioning of the shed rods is the final step before weaving. It is a simple procedure when one understands the purpose of each shed rod, as described above.

Needed: Ball of heddle string, seine twine or medium weight cotton. Minimum: 160".

1. *Upper Shed Rod:* This rod is already in position. It is the top of the two shed rods which were inserted to maintain the figure eight. This rod is left in its current position for it already separates alternate warps.

2. *Heddle Rod* or *Lower Shed Rod:* Lift lower shed rod until it is 6" beneath upper rod. In the area occupied by lower shed rod, insert first the batten and then the end of the heddle string. The insertion should be from right to left so the end of the string extends 2" out of the left side of the warp, and the ball of heddle string is free on

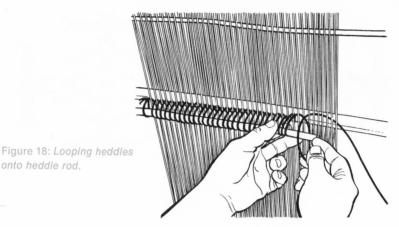

Figure 18: *Looping heddles onto heddle rod.*

the right side of the loom. Turn batten on edge and arrange string above. Remove rod from shed, and tie a 1″ loop in the left end of the heddle string.

You are now ready to arrange heddle loops on heddle rod.

Placing Heddle Loops Onto Heddle Rod (left to right):

　1. Hold heddle rod horizontally in left hand to the left of the warp and at the same level as the string. (The right end of the heddle rod should be at the left edge of the warp.)

　2. Insert right end of heddle rod into loop tied in end of string.

　3. With index and thumb of right hand, reach between first and second warps that cross the batten, grasp and pull the heddle string so as to create a 1½″ loop. Give loop a ¾ turn to the right and place the new loop onto the heddle rod next to the first one.

　4. Repeat procedure. With index finger and thumb of right hand, reach between the second and third warps that cross the batten, grasp and pull the heddle string so as to create a 1½″ loop. Give loop a ¾ turn to the right and place on the heddle rod next to the second loop.

　5. Repeat procedure across the loom, moving the rod to the right to accommodate each successive loop. Continue until all warps crossing the batten are looped and attached to the heddle rod. When the right edge is reached, once again tie a loop in the heddle string (as

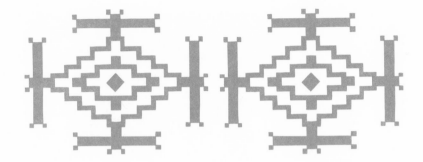

at the beginning), and insert the rod into this final loop. Any remaining string may be cut.

    6. Pull the heddle rod forward to make sure that every warp crossing the batten has been looped and none missed. If accurate, remove batten. If inaccurate, redo.

IX. INSTALL SIDE SELVAGE CORDS

Many Navajo weavings have side edging cords as well as end ones. These provide for long wear and are desirable especially on saddle blankets and floor rugs which get hard usage at edges. They are generally absent on wall tapestries and purses. For this project they are not recommended. Directions for use are in Appendix, and they should be set up at this time when weaving a project in which they are needed.

As a sort of "briefing" exercise, you may want to skim through this chapter now; then, once your weaving is underway, refer back to it. Whenever a problem occurs, check the chapter on *Remedies* at the end of the book to aid in determining the cause and correction. Some of the most common problems are briefly discussed here, in order that by being forewarned you may be able to avoid them completely.

Understanding the Shed Rods

You can now understand the workings of the Navajo loom. The very simple shed rods, which place alternate warps forward, are so elementary as to seem crude. And yet, you will undoubtedly marvel at such a direct solution and wonder how someone ever conceived of this answer to an age-old problem.

Play with the sheds a moment to celebrate your victory of warping. Push down the upper rod so that it lays on top of the heddle loops. Insert your batten in the space created, *below* the rods. Turn your batten on edge so as to widen the space.

The space you have created is called the "shed." This is essentially an opening between sets of warps, determined by the position of the shed rods, for the purpose of inserting weft. There are two positions for the shed rods: together or apart. The shed you just made with rods together is called the "stick-shed." The other one, the "pull-shed," is made when rods are apart. To do this, remove the batten stick. Push

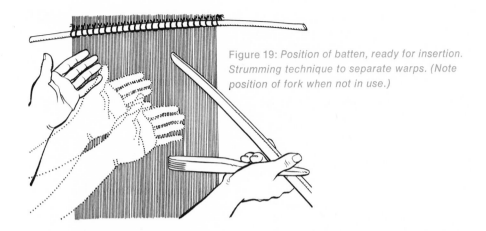

Figure 19: *Position of batten, ready for insertion. Strumming technique to separate warps. (Note position of fork when not in use.)*

the upper shed rod upward about a foot. Pull the heddle rod toward you far enough to bring the back warps to a frontal position. Insert your batten behind the heddles, turn it on edge and notice your alternate space for passage of weft.

By repeating these steps several times you will become acquainted with the workings of your Navajo loom. You will also note a few difficulties in inserting the batten. There are a few "secrets" which ease insertion. These are discussed in the next section.

Understanding the Batten

1. *Position of holding the batten:* With curved end to your left and longest edge up, grasp the batten with right hand at bottom center. The bottom of the batten should rest on the base of your index finger and again between fingertips of index and third fingers. (See figure 19.)

2. *Strum to separate warps:* If you are using wool warp, you will notice that the fibers of the warp sometimes stick together, hindering insertion of batten. If this is the case, strum the warp threads with backs of fingers of left hand (right to left). The vibration tends to separate warp strands and is a standard movement, especially before insertion in the "pull-shed." In the beginning, before the warp fibers have worn off, you may need to strum before inserting batten in both sheds.

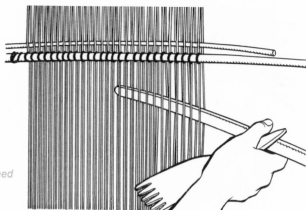

Figure 20: *Position of shed and heddle rods to create stick shed.*

3. *"Stick-shed":* Position shed rods together about halfway up the warp. Holding batten in above position, insert curved edge in opening between warps *below* shed rods. When batten is through and centered, reach up with both hands, grasp ends and turn on edge so that the top of the batten is toward you. (See figure 23.)

4. *Removal of batten:* Return batten to flat position, grasp right end with right hand, and pull out. This procedure can be further refined by pulling batten just half-way out and then transferring grasp to bottom center for remaining pull. In this way the batten will be in correct position for next insertion, and weaving will be hastened.

5. *Retain batten in hand while changing shed:* Do not put batten down between shed changes, for you will have to relocate it, pick it up again and reposition it in your hand. Much time will be lost and the weaving process lengthened. It is considered the mark of a skilled weaver to retain weaving tools in hand when not in use. An additional advantage is that of insuring an unbroken weaving rhythm.

6. *"Pull-shed":* Push upper shed upward, about 6″ above lower rod. With left hand strum warps (see step 2), then grasp heddle rod near right edge (see figure 21). Firmly pull rod so back warps will come to front position. With batten held in position described above (step 1) insert it between warps as far as it will comfortably go, release left hand, grasp heddle rod further to left, pull forward again, and continue to insert batten. This may be repeated across the loom

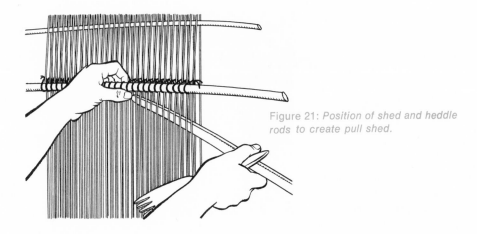

Figure 21: *Position of shed and heddle rods to create pull shed.*

until batten is all the way through. The number of times needed to grasp, pull, and release the heddle rod depends on:

    a. width of your rug

    b. how well you separated your warps by strumming

    c. how far you are on your weaving (more toward the end)

    d. the precision with which your batten curves

Understanding the Fork

The fork is the final tool to be reckoned with.

Its position when in use: Approaching fork from right, grasp with right hand at a point just before the handle tapers. Place thumb beneath and fingers on top. (See figure 22.)

The rhythm of the fork is a flicking wrist action, pushed down by the top fingers. It flutters along the weaving line, beating the weft strands into position. It is also used to separate warp strands if they ease too close together (see chapter on *Remedies*).

The main thing to learn in using the fork is to retain it in your hand at all times. Its position when in use is described above. Its position when "at rest" is as follows:

Turn fork tines downward out of the way. In this position it is held against the heel of the hand by the fourth and fiftn fingers. This leaves the first three fingers free to grasp batten. The position can be seen in the figure above and in figure 19.

Navajo children learning to weave are sometimes admonished about putting the fork down:

> *My mother always used to watch me weave. And when I didn't need the fork I would put it down and than pick it up again when I needed it. And my mother would say, "You just have to keep it in your hand all the time. When you get married, your mother-in-law will see you put it down and she will say:*
>
> *"Let's just chase this girl away from here, she doesn't even know how to weave."*
>
> *And even after she told me that, for a long time I still would lay it down, and my mother would always remind me. And sometimes I would just tell her,*
>
> *"It just slipped from my hand," or "I just put it down because I'm going to stop weaving for a while."*

Understanding the Navajo Count

When a Navajo says, "This design should be two warps here," she means *two pair* or four actual threads by Anglo thinking. A Navajo weaver always counts her pattern by inserting the batten and counting the warps that cross it.

This method results in each element of the design containing an

even number of warp threads, for even if a weaver says, "Three warps here," she is referring to three pair, and hence six strands.

Such an approach determines a certain design proportion, as well as uniformly made joints; in addition, since only half the number of warp threads are considered, it is easier to remember a design.

How to Mark the Centers

Since most Navajo designs are laterally and vertically symmetrical, marking the center in both directions is one of the first steps to follow setting up the loom.

MARKING THE LATERAL CENTER

The Navajo weaver in determining the lateral center inserts the batten in the "stick-shed" and counts warps from each side until she arrives in the center. She then loosely encircles the center warp(s) by tying a piece of string around two center warps (when she is working with an even number of warps). She then pushes the string up to the top of the weaving, out of the way. A marked center is extremely helpful when weaving a pattern where much warp counting is required.

MARKING THE VERTICAL CENTER

The Navajo weaver, after tightening her warp, takes a piece of string

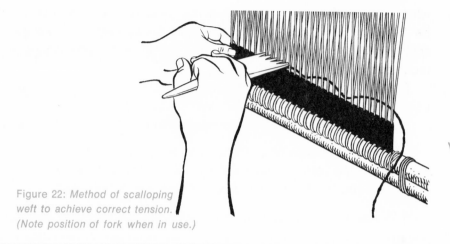

Figure 22: *Method of scalloping weft to achieve correct tension. (Note position of fork when in use.)*

and measures the height of her warp. She then folds this carefully in half and uses this to gauge the vertical center of the rug. At this point she makes a *dark* line with whatever is handy (crayon, pen, felt tip, etc.) on the four center warps.

If each half will contain a complete design, she again folds the doubled string in half and makes a mark at one-quarter and three-quarters of the warp height. As she weaves, these marks help her gauge her progress in achieving symmetry.

A measuring tape is equally effective in determining and marking the vertical and lateral centers.

How to Regulate Weft Tension

A surprisingly large part of the skill of Navajo weaving comes with learning the appropriate tension to be used with the weft. Many of the problems that occur in Navajo weaving are the result of incon-sistent and inappropriate weft tension. It is for this reason that we are fully describing the methods of arriving at correct tension, and means of determining when the tension is correct.

Method A: *Scallops* or *Bubbling*

In this method, weft is drawn through the shed and then at intervals pressed with fingers or point of fork to the weaving line, which results in scallops. The size of the scallop determines the amount of weft which will be beaten in place with the fork. The scallop should not be too high as excess weft will result. Conversely, too shallow a scallop will result in tightness. A rule of thumb to use with the scallop technique is:

For a weaving 10″ wide, four scallops can be made, the peak of each about ¾″ from the weaving line;

or, each 10″ of weaving area requires an approximate 12″ of weft.

The above rule cannot be used as an absolute measure, as the size and spin of the yarn is also a determining factor. Instead, we recommend that you try the above rule, and then watch the results.

1. If any of the following are happening you are probably *not using enough weft* in the shed. Remedy: Take out what you have woven and as you reweave, increase the height of the scallops.

    a. Warp is showing between weft that was put in a few rows back.

    b. Side selvages are beginning to pull inward.

    c. Warps are becoming too close in some areas.

2. If any of the following are happening you are probably *using too much weft* in the shed. Remedy: Take out what you have woven and reduce height of scallops.

    a. Loops are being formed on the front or rear of the fabric.

    b. When edges of fabric are pulled outward, a great elasticity is present and fabric expands more than ½″ overall.

    c. Selvage edges are being pushed out more than the intended width of the project.

NOTE: IT IS EASIER TO INCLUDE TOO LITTLE WEFT THAN TO INCLUDE TOO MUCH. IF YOU ARE UNCERTAIN AS TO YOUR TENSION, IT IS BETTER TO THINK *LOOSE.*

3. If the following is happening, your tension is probably uneven: Sometimes too loose, and sometimes too tight. Remedy: Once again take out your weaving back to where the trouble began and reweave, having learned from the experience.

    a. Material is rippling, due to area of tight tension followed by areas of loose tension.

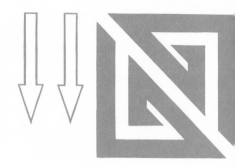

Method B. *Hitting the Bound Edge*

Most proficient Navajo weavers do not bother creating scallops. They have a feeling in their fingers for how much and when they should pull on the weft.

We suggest that when you are laying in a striped area, or a large design, you use the scallop. When you are creating a section of more intricate design, an alternate method, that of hitting the bound edge, may be effective.

Procedure: If the yarn is going from right to left, hold the free end of the weft diagonally with left hand and pack with fork, using a right-to-left progression so that the bound end of the weft is hit first. The procedure is reversed when the weft is traveling from left to right.

In this method it is important to notice the amount of tension applied by the hand holding the free end, also the angle at which the yarn is being held. The same criteria for tension, presented in the scallop method, are appropriate to apply here.

How to Keep Edges Straight

One of the most easily recognizable indications that a rug was made by an accomplished weaver is the straight selvage edges. The reverse is also true of the novice. If tension of weft is mastered and if warp is kept tightly strung, this problem usually never appears. It is because

the edges are one of the most exasperating aspects for any beginning weaver, that we refer you in advance to the section on *Remedies* at the back of the book, in which causes and corrections of this irritating phenomenon are fully described. *Measure the width of your weaving frequently* and at slightest deviation, turn to chapter on *Remedies.*

How to Fill in Low Spots

In order for a stripe to be crisp and straight, the base on which it is placed must be straight. We have therefore presented a full discussion on keeping the weaving line straight and filling in low spots in the back of the book under *Remedies.* Be forewarned and encouraged, however, that if your weft was selected for its uniformity of size and spin, and if your warp is kept tight and hence evenly spaced, your problems here will be nominal.

How to Keep Warps Evenly Spaced

The first step in keeping warps evenly spaced is the edging cord, which determines initial spacing.

The second step is the binding cord and the tightness with which it was bound. This stabilizes the spacing.

The third step is the tension of the warp, which is responsible for maintaining the correct spacing. If the warp is tight, incorrect weft

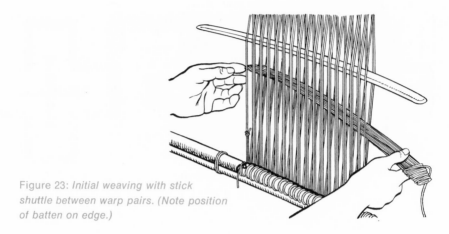

Figure 23: *Initial weaving with stick shuttle between warp pairs. (Note position of batten on edge.)*

tension or inconsistent size of weft will not move it unduly.

If you are having difficulty with this aspect, the chapter on *Remedies* may once again be of help to you in correcting the problem.

How to Make the Stick Shuttle

Navajo weaving with its intricate designs requires that colors be hooked and pieced together to create the multifaceted whole. Only where one color crosses the entire weaving width, as in a stripe, is a shuttle used. In such instances the shuttle is made by breaking a straight stick from the native greasewood (*diwuzhi*) and allowing it to dry. Ends are not smoothed. The average stick is about 28″ long but any size will do, the shuttle being easier to grasp when the stick length exceeds the width of the weaving.

Substitution: Any straight stick with a broken end may be used for the shuttle. A small dowel or a plastic "pick-up-shuttle" such as used in Anglo weaving will also do.

Winding the Stick Shuttle

1. Hold yarn end between index finger and thumb of left hand and twirl rough end of stick in end of yarn to catch and hold it.

2. Wrap end of stick securely three times.

3. Using five long wraps, circle the stick and arrive at opposite end. Again wrap securely three times.

4. Repeat process of five long wraps to reach first end, giving three more tight wraps below primary wrapping.

5. Continue process until you have carried the yarn to one end and back, five times. Break yarn about 20″ from tip last wrapped.

Usage: When weaving a stripe, adequate yarn to cross the entire weaving width may be unwound from the stick shuttle, shuttle inserted through shed, and yarn packed in place.

How to Break the Weft

Navajo yarn is always broken — never cut. This gives the yarn end a natural taper and is useful in two stages of weaving. When you run out of yarn and want to add a piece, the joints will be imperceptible if the ends are tapered. Again, when you want to secure the end of a new color to start a design, the tapered end will make the job easier.

To break Navajo yarn, grasp wool between thumb and index finger of each hand, with hands 2″ apart. Untwist the yarn, rolling counter to spin, then pull apart.

How to Piece Yarn Within a Design

When yarn runs out within a stripe or design, no knot is used to connect the old with the new. Instead, *ends are overlapped about 1″ and the weaving continued in the same direction.* If the ends were broken and hence are tapered, the joint will be imperceptible.

How to Weave the First and Last Four Rows

The first and last 4 rows of the weaving require special treatment, the purpose being to hide warps which at this point are bound in pairs. The count for these rows is: Over the first warp, then under 2, over 2, under 2, etc., for the rest of the row. In each instance the "2" are a bound pair (extensions of a warp turn). The procedure for executing these 4 rows is described in further detail in the following chapter.

How to Gauge Vertical Distances

When a stripe or design has reached the desired height (judged visually), weave 2 or more rows and begin with the new color. The extra rows are used to counter the additional packing which occurs when subsequent wefts are beaten down.

How to Lay-In a Yarn

When it is time to lay-in your first weft, or any weft for a new design, do not allow the initial end to hang out. Rather, pull the yarn through the shed until the naturally tapered end is just inside the design area.

Initial ends that are left to hang out require a great deal of work to reincorporate into the weaving upon completion of the project. Even worse is the snipping-off treatment, as these blunt ends will work their way out and come loose.

Navajo weavers who leave the ends hanging out in order to simplify the process and hasten the product, are not considered to be good weavers by their peers.

Beginning to Weave

You have undoubtedly been thinking about design and have visions of the many beautiful Navajo rugs you have seen. Because beginning weavers may be overwhelmed by the multiplicity of choices, we offer some suggestions for your first weaving.

Traditionally the first weaving a Navajo weaver makes is striped. This is a practical idea as it allows the young girl to get used to a loom and its technicalities and removes many of the complications created by a weaver trying too complicated a design before she is ready. There are lovely first rugs, woven in stripes with many colors. Sometimes each band is a uniform width and the colors vary. Sometimes the bands are of various widths. A well-woven striped rug is a thing of beauty.

The Navajo seem to be endowed with a great patience. They look forward to the many more rugs they will create. They have a faith in the future. They can make a striped first rug.

Some weavers may not wish to be traditionally Navajo in their first design, and for these weavers, eager to try out everything and anything — preferably all at once — we present a composite pattern.

The pattern we have selected (shown on page 57) combines the best of both approaches. It has its share of stripes as well as the fun of design.

It can be carried out in bright dramatic colors or soft plant-dyed hues with equal effectiveness.

In addition, it has a few strategic possibilities to help a weaver-of-a-first-project:

1. This design starts with a band of solid color just when you are cautious and trying to get used to the loom. Then, when you are getting the feeling of the technique and rhythm, it eases first into a vertical, then into a diagonal. By then you will be a virtuoso!

2. At the center of the weaving there is another strategic stripe — a highly functional maneuver to take up any slack if the bottom design suddenly looks like it's going to come out too small or too large. It also has a psychological importance — it allows you to make great forward strides just when things start slowing down.

3. From the center stripe forward you are on your own. You *can* repeat the same design and color scheme if you wish. But if this weaving will ultimately be a purse or container, you open the doors to *many* more possibilities. In such a situation both sides will not be seen at one and the same time. *Therefore:*

   a. You may want to keep the same design and change colors — for a new look and new interest.
   b. You may want to keep the same colors for unity and change the design, utilizing one of the designs in this book that caught your fancy.
   c. You may want to change everything — design *and* color — for a whole new feeling!

In any case, decide on a design for the second half which is interesting to you so you will be motivated to continue and finish the weaving. "Psych yourself out" so you will not leave the weaving in a partially completed state.

Design Considerations

Traditional Navajo designs are handed down from generation to generation, with some innovation by each weaver. As a result, some rug designs have reached a certain refinement and precision of balance, color and proportion . . . a refinement possible only by repetition over time. From watching grandmother do it, then mother do it, and then doing it oneself, the design becomes "memorized" — by string count usually.

57

Sometimes two patterns are combined — the border of one rug with the internal design of another. In such instances, there are certain principles a weaver may apply to the designing process. Just as unity is of concern to artists of any medium and culture, so Navajo weavers may point out that the border should relate to the central design. If vertical joints are used in one, then vertical joints should be present in the other.

You may want to let the principle of unity guide you when you make up the second half of your design. You may also find it helpful to graph your design before weaving it. A line can represent two warps, or as a Navajo counts, *one* (pair).

58   THE PROJECT: Step-by-Step Instructions

The following is a diagram of the 10″ x 23″ design suggested for your first project. A numeral indicates each innovation of design or technique. The drawing and numerals will be referred to throughout the following directions.

Before you begin weaving: Warp the loom, tighten the warp and then mark the 4 center warps to indicate one-fourth, one-half and three quarters of the length. Also find and encircle the center warps (see *Weaving Basics,* page 47).

The initial yellow stripe is 1½″. All vertical distances in the white shape are ½″. This project requires approximately ½ lb. of weft. For the colors shown here you will need ¼ lb. of brown, ¼ lb. of white; ½ oz. orange for cross, and 2 ozs. yellow for stripes.

 FIRST FOUR ROWS

The first four rows of a weaving require special treatment to provide complete coverage of the warps which here are bound in pairs. Shed rods are pushed up out of the way as they are not used in this process.

Wrap a stick-shuttle with yellow yarn (see chapter on *Weaving Basics,* page 52).

Row 1: Lay-in beginning weft

1. From right to left, insert the larger 1″ batten between the warp pairs as follows: Behind the first warp, in front of the second *pair,*

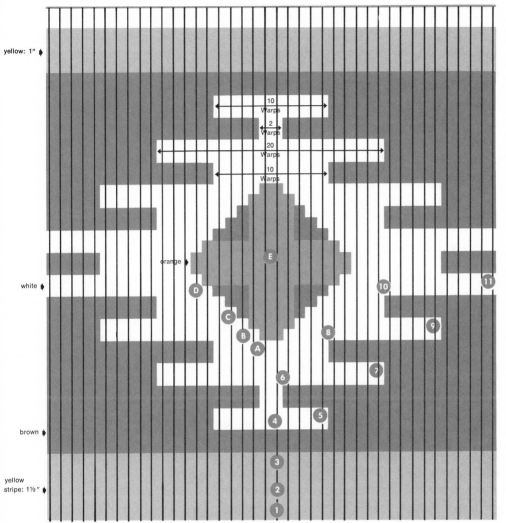

yellow: 1″

10 Warps

2 Warps

20 Warps

10 Warps

orange

white

brown

yellow stripe: 1½″

E

D

C

B

A

10

11

8

9

7

6

5

4

3

2

1

Vertical black lines represent individual warps. There are forty.
The initial yellow stripe is 1½″. All vertical distances in the
white shape are ½″.

behind the third *pair,* etc. This count continues until the batten spans the full width of the rug. The batten should end up in back of the last warp. Turn batten on edge.

2. From right to left, insert stick-shuttle with yellow yarn in space provided *below* batten. Grasp shuttle on left side of warp with left hand. Pull through until the end of the yellow yarn is just inside the right edge of the warp. This is the method of *laying-in a new color* (see *Weaving Basics,* page 54), and will be referred to in future directions.

3. From right to left, arrange yarn in scallops (see chapter on *Weaving Basics,* page 48).

4. Beat weft securely in place with fork. Start at right side and progress to left, using a tamping rhythm. Remove batten.

60   *Row 2: Reverse direction of weft*

1. From right to left insert batten using the opposite count: In front of the first warp, behind the second pair, in front of the third pair, etc. Turn batten on edge.

2. From left to right insert the stick-shuttle with yellow yarn through shed. Pull through to right side, carefully allowing weft to encircle left outside warp softly. Arrange yellow weft in scallops.

3. Beat weft in place, starting at left side and working to your right across the weaving line.

Rows 3 and 4 are the same as 1 and 2.

Note: Be cautious with the edges. In an effort to create an even selvage, weavers often pull too tight on the weft as it encircles the edge warp. This causes edges to go in. Leave the encircling weft loose enough to comfortably encircle side warp without displacing it, but tight enough not to create a large edge loop.

Lessons Derived Thus Far:

1. TO LAY-IN NEW YARN: *Trail weft through until tapered yarn end is just inside specified area.*

2. TO CREATE EVEN SELVAGES: *Encircle edge warps loosely with the weft.*

3. TO BEAT WEFT IN PLACE WITH FORK: *Always start at the bound edge.*

2 ROW 5 AND ONWARD: USE REGULAR SHEDS

Upon completion of first four rows, the yellow yarn should be hanging from the right side of the warp. Row 5 starts the use of shed rods.

Row 5:

Arrange shed rods together to create the "stick-shed." Strum. Insert batten and turn on edge. From right to left, insert stick-shuttle with yellow weft, pull through, arrange in scallops, and beat into place with the fork.

Row 6:

Arrange shed and heddle rods apart to create "pull-shed." Strum. Pull heddle rod. Insert batten; turn batten on edge; insert stick-shuttle from left to right; arrange weft in scallops and beat into place.

Rows 5 and 6:

Repeat until the yellow stripe is 1½" wide. If during the weaving of the stripe, the yellow yarn runs out, rewind stick-shuttle and continue weaving *in the same direction* you were going, letting yarn ends overlap about 1".

When stripe is 1½" wide, weave in 2 more rows to compensate for future packing. Finish with yarn hanging at right.

Additional Lesson Derived:

TO PIECE YARN: *Overlap ends 1" and continue weaving in the same direction.*

3 COLOR CHANGE

When yellow stripe is just past 1½" in width, it is time to begin the brown background.

1. The first step is to check to see if weaving row is even, and no low spots are occurring. If there are irregularities, fill in the low spots, using technique described in *Remedies* (page 84). An even weaving row assures the next color of having a straight base.

2. With yarn hanging from right side of warp, break off about 6" from the edge.

3. Wind stick-shuttle with brown yarn.

4. With batten in "stick-shed" insert the final 6" of yellow yarn into shed (right to left).

61

5. Insert stick-shuttle with brown yarn in *same direction* pulling the yarn end through until the brown yarn overlaps the yellow by one inch.

6. Continue weaving as before, until you have woven a brown stripe which will be ½″ in the finished project.

Take Stock: Upon completion of the brown stripe consider the following to see how you have mastered the method thus far.

1. Are your edges going in? Measure the width of the weaving to see if it deviates from the planned 10″.

2. Are the warp threads showing through the weft?

3. Are there any low spots along the weaving line?

If any of the above characteristics are present, turn to chapter on *Remedies* to ascertain correction.

④ INTRODUCING DESIGN (with vertical joint)

You are now 2″ along on your project. If you are having much difficulty with the method thus far, you may want to redesign your weaving and continue with stripes.

If you are satisfied with your progress and understanding, begin introducing design.

Initial-Design-Shed:

Before beginning your design you need to decide in which direction and in which shed to start your design. For purposes of clarity we will call this your "initial-design-shed."

This will set you on a course of weaving in which your design will have the same number of warps in the stick-shed as are in the pull-shed.

How to determine your "initial-design-shed":

Your first row of design must have the weft going *right to left* in the shed that places the *left edge warp in forward position* (in front of the batten).

If you have been following directions so far, you will find that your yarn is hanging at the right of your weaving. Your batten will be placed in the "stick-shed" which holds the left edge warp forward. In this instance, the initial-design-shed involves starting your design right to left in the "stick-shed." Proceed to Row 1 of the design directions.

If in subsequent weavings you find that with your yarns hanging at right of the weaving and the batten in your initial-design-shed, this is the same shed you have just used to arrive at the right, follow these steps to change weft direction:

1. Break off yarn 1″ inside right edge of weaving.
2. Insert batten in "initial-design-shed."
3. Lay-in yarn right to left, so end of yarn is inside left edge of weaving, about 2″.
4. Insert batten in opposite shed. Weave weft left to right for entire row.

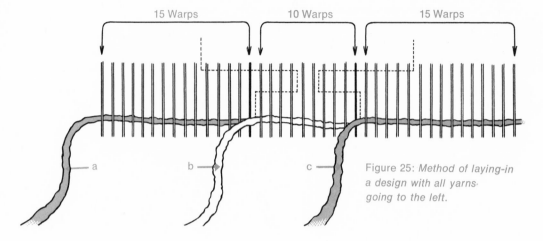

a   b   c   Figure 25: *Method of laying-in a design with all yarns going to the left.*

64

5. Yarn will now be hanging at right of weaving and your next row to left will be that of laying out your design in the "initial-design-shed."

LAYING-IN A DESIGN (with vertical joint)

You are now beginning a white design that has vertical sides. The joint between brown and white yarns used here is the "hooked joint." See Appendix for alternate methods.

Row 1:

1. With brown yarn hanging at right side of weaving, insert batten in "stick-shed" (your initial-design-shed).

2. Count warps to determine the *center 10.* Remember that the Navajo weaver counts only those warps which cross the batten. When the center 10 are located, recheck by counting the warps on each side. There should be 15. (You can put little pieces of yarn between warps to mark your place while counting.)

3. The 40 warps which cross the batten are now divided into three warp sections: 15, 10, 15 warps each. You are now ready to lay-in the design.

    a. Break off brown yarn about 15″ from warp. Break off another piece of brown yarn also about 15″ and "lay-it-in" from right to left just behind the 15 warps on the left side of your warp. Pull this through until the end does not stick out of the right side of the 15 warp section.

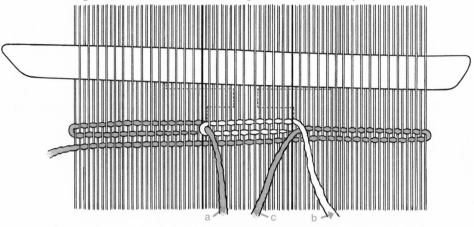

b. Break off a comparable piece of white yarn. Still weaving right to left, "lay-it-in" behind the center 10 warps.

c. In the same way, insert the existing brown yarn hanging at the right side of the weaving, through the shed from right to left, passing only behind the 15 warps on the right side of the weaving.

These pieces of yarn should be scalloped and beaten into position with the fork.

Row 2:

At this time there are three yarn ends hanging from the weaving line: two brown ones and a white one in between. All three were woven right to left; thus their free ends hang at the left of their design area.

In order that the colors be firmly joined together in the final product, each color is hooked to its neighbor as it travels back across the weaving:

a. Insert batten in "pull-shed." With fingers of left hand, pick up brown yarn hanging on left side of warp, and insert it through the shed behind the 15 warps that cross the batten. Beat in place.

b. Arrange this brown yarn so that it *crosses on top* of the adjacent white yarn. With left hand, pick up white yarn coming from *beneath* the brown, insert it behind the center 10 warps and out (left to right). As before, cross this white yarn over the adjacent brown yarn.

    c. The brown yarn then completes the row, coming from beneath the white, behind its own 15 warps and is beaten in place.

The second row of design is thus completed. Note that *hooking has occurred in the "pull-shed."*

A suggestion on hooking this vertical joint: When going left to right, pull hooked weft tightly to make a compact joint. Make certain, however, you do not pull so tightly that you displace warp threads. Once the weft is past the joint it can be beaten in loosely.

Row 3:

Set-up: Three yarns hanging at right sides of designs. Batten in "stick-shed."

1. Starting on left side as you do when you read, the left brown yarn reverses its direction going to the left (15 warps). Then the white one does the same (10 warps). Finally the right brown yarn finishes the row (15 warps).

2. Note that in the "stick-shed" the yarns do not hook around each other, as they are already hooked from previous row.

3. Note also that all yarns travel in the same direction through one shed. When the shed changes, all yarns as though acting as one, reverse and create the next row.

4. Note further that at the beginning of each new row, the yarn on the far left is the first to be used, regardless of which direction you are going, and regardless of which shed you are using.

From these observations we can form additional rules which will apply to this project.

1. *Hook yarns only when in "pull-shed."*

2. *Keep all yarns going in same direction throughout a row.*

3. *For each row, always use the yarn on the far left first.*

4. *For design, use pieces of yarn about 15" in length.*

Row 4:

The fourth row of design is identical to the second. Continue to form the design, by weaving each color back and forth over its own territory. Do this until the white design is just over ½" wide. It will probably take about 6 more rows, depending on size of weft (10–12 in all). In finished weaving it will appear as 5–6 joints at edge of design.

When you have determined how many rows your weft requires to form ½", you can use the same number of rows for each section of the design that is ½".

5 CHANGE VERTICAL DESIGN
New Count: Brown 19 • White 2 • Brown 19

When white design is just over ½", it is time to decrease center area of white while simultaneously expanding the side areas of brown (see diagram of design).

Row 1:

67

Set-up: Three yarn ends hanging at right of designs. Batten in "stick-shed."

1. Weave left brown yarn to left edge as before (15 warps).

2. Weave center white yarn to left for 6 warp threads.

3. Weave right brown yarn to left for 19 warps. (This is 4 past the regular 15.)

At this point you will notice that the white is contracting and the brown is expanding

Row 2:

Set-up: Three yarn ends hanging at left of designs. Batten in the "pull-shed."

1. Weave left brown yarn to right 19 warps (4 past regular 15). Hook brown with adjacent white yarn.

2. Weave white yarn to right for 2 warps, and hook with waiting brown yarn.

3. Weave right brown yarn to right edge for the remaining 19 warps. The new count is thus set up. Continue design for ½".

Two lessons can be distilled from the above technique:

1. Only decrease or advance the count in one direction at a time.

2. It takes two rows (one to the left, then back to the right) *to set up a design change.*

6 CHANGE VERTICAL DESIGN
New Count: Brown 10   •   White 20   •   Brown 10

Row 1:

Set-up: Three yarns hanging at right of designs. Batten in the "stick-shed."
1. Weave left brown yarn to left edge as before (19 warps.)
2. Weave center white yarn 11 warps to left (9 past the 2). At this point white will be on top of brown in same shed.
3. Weave right brown yarn 10 warps to left.

Row 2:

Set-up: Three yarn ends hanging at left of designs. Batten in the "pull-shed."
1. Weave left brown yarn 10 warps to right. Hook with white.
2. Weave center white yarn 20 warps to right. Hook with brown.
3. Weave right brown yarn to right edge (10 warps).

7 CHANGE VERTICAL DESIGN
New Count: Brown 15   •   White 10   •   Brown 15

Set-up: Three yarns hanging at right of designs. Batten in the "stick-shed."
1. Weave left brown yarn to left edge (10 warps).
2. Weave center white yarn 15 warps to left (5 less).
3. Weave right brown yarn 15 warps to left (5 more).

Row 2:

Set-up: Three yarn ends hanging at left of designs. Batten in the "pull-shed."
1. Weave left brown yarn 15 warps to right. Hook with white.
2. Weave center white yarn 10 warps to right. Hook with brown.
3. Weave right brown yarn to right edge, to complete row.
Continue design for ½".

8 CHANGE VERTICAL DESIGN
New Count: Brown 5   •   White 30   •   Brown 5

Row 1:

Set-up: Three yarn ends hanging at right of designs. Batten in the "stick-shed."

1. Weave left brown yarn 15 warps to left.
2. Weave center white yarn 20 warps to left.
3. Weave right brown yarn 5 warps to left.

Row 2:

Set-up: Three yarn ends hanging at left of designs. Batten in the "pull-shed."

1. Weave left brown yarn 5 warps to right. Hook with white yarn.
2. Weave center white yarn 30 warps to right. Hook with brown.
3. Weave right brown yarn to right edge (5 warps).

Stop here and take stock before continuing to next row which will begin the laying-in of diagonal design. (You are now at "A" on the drawing.)

Take Stock: Consider the following to see how well you have mastered the vertical design joint.

1. Are your edges going in? Measure width of weaving to see if it deviates from the planned 10 inches.
2. Are warp threads showing through the weft?
3. Are there any low spots along the weaving line? Are any horizontal design lines wavering?
4. Are there heavy ridges along the vertical design joints?
5. Are warp threads too close together in any one location?

If any of the above characteristics are present, turn to the chapter on *Remedies* to ascertain correction.

You have now completed just over 4″ of your weaving. If the technique thus far has been difficult and you would like more time to master the vertical designs, we suggest you continue just the main large white shape and omit the center diamond.

If, however, you are pleased with your results thus far and are eager for more challenge, go ahead with the diamond now. Directions are in the following section.

Because there is so much difference in weaving approaches (some people pack harder than others, some use heavier yarn, some space warp further, etc.), we will not try to coordinate the diamond with the white shape for you. Instead, we will give you measurements. At the time your design reaches the given size, proceed to the next step.

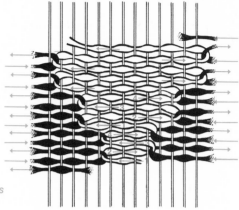

Figure 27: *Detail of hooked wefts in stepped edge diamond.*

Completion of Large White Design

9 When you get to 9 on the drawing, it will be time to reduce the white shape 5 warps on each side, for ½". The white shape will have the same boundaries as it did at 6.

10 When you get to 10 on the drawing, it will be time to expand the white to the edges on the weaving. This part of the design is also continued for ½".

11 At 11 on the drawing, brown is again laid in for 5 warps on each side, just as it was at 9. During this block of color, you will reach the middle and can reverse the design.

In all instances in which you are enlarging or reducing the design, follow this routine:

1. Start with all yarn ends hanging on the right of the design area.

2. Insert batten in "stick-shed."

3. Weave entire row from right to left and extend or decrease the design in this direction first.

4. When all yarns hang from left of design, change to "pull-shed" and weave entire row left to right, making final adjustments in designs.

WEAVING DIAGONAL PATTERN

There are many variations in weaving the diagonal pattern. The technique you select is based on how steep an angle your design

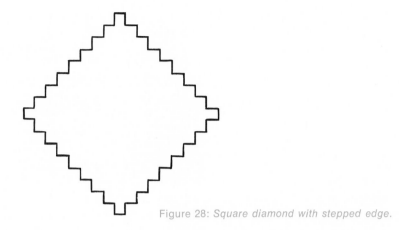

Figure 28: *Square diamond with stepped edge.*

requires, as well as how strong a joint is needed. These variations and considerations are discussed in the Appendix.

The diagonal design chosen for this project is the square diamond with the stepped edge. The hooked joint will again be used, as it provides the greatest strength.

The stepped edge on the square diamond requires essentially the same technique you have been using. The main difference is that each *step* is not repeated for long. Instead, the shape is first expanded and then decreased on a regular basis to form the diamond. The accompanying diagram depicts this expansion: *First expand to the left, then to the right,* just as you have been doing in the white design. After the 2 expansion rows, there are *2 rows woven in place. A total of 4 rows constitutes one step.* If your yarn is small and 4 rows do not make ¼", then weave until this height is reached.

Ⓐ LAYING-IN DIAGONAL PATTERN *(First Step of Stepped Edge)*
   Diamond Count: Orange 2

Row 1:

   Set-up: Three yarn ends hanging from right of designs. Batten in "stick-shed."

   1. Weave left brown yarn to left edge.
   2. Break off piece of white yarn. Lay it (right to left) behind the

next 14 warps. (It will begin just left of the 2 center warps and continue to edge of white.)

 3. Break off a piece of orange yarn. Lay-it-in (right to left) behind the 2 center warps.

 4. Weave existing white yarn up to the beginning of the orange yarn.

 5. Weave final brown yarn to the left 5 warps to await white on return row.

Row 2:

 Set-up: Five yarn ends hanging at left of designs. Batten in the "pull-shed."

 1. Weave brown yarn to right. Hook with white.

 2. Weave white to the right. Hook with orange.

 3. Weave orange to the right. Hook with white.

 4. Weave white to right. Hook with brown.

 5. Weave brown to the right edge.

Rows 3 and 4 (of this *First Step*):

 Continue with the same count for 2 more rows and then proceed to next directions.

B DIAGONAL PATTERN *(Second Step of Stepped Edge)*

Expanding the diamond one warp on each side. The count of the orange will be *4 warps.*

Row 1:

 Set-up: Five yarn ends hanging to the right of designs. Batten in "stick-shed."

 1. Weave left brown yarn to left edge.

 2. Weave white yarn to left.

 3. *Weave center orange yarn to left 3 warps.*

 4. Weave right white yarn to orange, less one warp.

 5. Weave brown yarn to left — up to white.

Row 2:

 Set-up: Five yarn ends hanging to left of designs. Batten in the "pull-shed."

 1. Weave left brown yarn to right. Hook with white.

 2. Weave white yarn to right. Hook with orange.

 3. *Weave orange yarn to right for 4 warps. Hook with white.*

4. Weave white yarn to right. Hook with brown.

5. Weave brown yarn to right edge.

Rows 3 and 4:

Weave 2 more rows continuing the orange with 4 warps. Then proceed to C.

If you prefer to simplify the design and technique, you may want to make the entire diamond orange instead of embellishing it with the cross.

If things seem to be going well, however, it is time to start the brown background of the diamond.

In either case, keep in mind the height of the white design you are currently making. When it is ½", decrease 5 warps on each side as described in step 9 on the drawing.

Ⓒ BROWN BACKGROUND DIAMOND *(Third Step of Stepped Edge)*

Addition of brown background expands the diamond one warp on each side.

You will notice that the orange yarn in the center is now 4 warps wide, which is the full width of the cross base. The orange yarn will stay at this width for the next inch, until about ⅜" from the one-quarter mark. The *brown background* around the cross is the next aspect to receive attention. It is begun at this time and will *continue the diagonal steps started by the orange.*

Row 1:

Diamond Count: Brown 1   •   Orange 4   •   Brown 1

Set-up: Five yarn ends hanging at right of the designs. Batten in "stick-shed."

1. Weave left brown yarn to left edge.

2. Weave white yarn to left, distance depending on development of white design.

3. *Lay-in new brown yarn behind one warp.* It is the warp on the left of the orange area. (Counting warps from left this would be warp No. 18.) Anchor tapered end of brown by winding it counter-clockwise around this warp 2 times.

4. Weave orange yarn to left 4 warps.

5. *Lay-in another brown yarn behind one warp,* on right side of

orange. (Counting from the right edge this would be warp No. 18.) Anchor end as before.

6. Weave existing white yarn to left up to new brown.

7. Weave existing brown yarn to left, distance depending on development of white design.

You now have 7 yarns hanging at left of their designs. Insert batten in "pull-shed."

1. Weave left brown yarn to right. Hook with white.

2. Weave white yarn to right. Hook with brown.

3. *Weave new brown yarn to right one warp. Hook with orange.*

4. *Weave orange yarn to right 4 warps. Hook with brown.*

5. *Weave brown yarn to right one warp. Hook with white.*

6. Weave white yarn to right. Hook with brown.

7. Weave brown yarn to right edge.

Weave two more rows to finish the *Third Step.*

When this *Step* is 4 rows (or ¼") once again expand the diamond one warp on each side as before. Continue with each step until you are about ⅜" from your middle mark, at which time you will be ready for D.

Guide for Increasing Steps:

First row: Yarns will go right to left in "stick-shed." Increase left diamond yarn one warp to left. Decrease right white yarn one warp to the left.

Second row: Yarns will go left to right to "pull-shed." Left white yarn meets diamond yarn by going one warp less. Right diamond yarn meets right white yarn by going one more warp.

Do not forget to extend your white shape clear to the edge when it reaches 10 on the drawing.

Discontinuation of Yarns

At this time the side brown yarns will be temporarily discontinued. Break left one 1" from weaving and weave stub to left. White yarn will go right on top of it and past. Once the row is complete do the same with the right edge brown yarn before it begins to the left.

Ⓓ EXTENDING ARMS OF CROSS

When you are about ⅜" from the middle of your design, it is time to extend the orange arms of the cross and thus add another *step* to the diamond.

Row 1:

The left brown diamond yarn will be discontinued. Therefore break it 1″ from the weaving and insert it in the "stick-shed."

Begin the row by weaving the white yarn clear to the left edge.

Follow with the orange yarn which goes one warp past the entire brown area to establish a new *Step.*

The remaining brown yarn follows as usual.

The last white yarn should stop one warp short of the brown section to await expansion of the orange in the next row.

Row 2:

The remaining brown diamond yarn will be discontinued. Therefore break it 1″ from the weaving and insert end in the "pull-shed."

Begin row at left: Weave white to right to connect with orange.

Orange crosses its own and the brown section, plus one warp further to make new *Step.* It hooks with white and white completes row.

At end of this row you will have only 3 yarns hanging from the weaving.

Repeat process for Rows 3 and 4. When these 4 rows are complete add final *Step* to the diamond, expanding one warp in each direction.

Continue weaving toward middle of the design. When you are ¼″ from your mark it is time to add brown yarn to the edges for 5 warps.

E MIDDLE OF THE DESIGN

When you are at your mark, you will have completed one-fourth of your weaving. In finishing the design, consult with the drawing and the first half of your weaving to determine count. This half will proceed much more quickly as you will be more certain of the process and will not need to refer to the directions as frequently. Perhaps not at all.

Guide to Decreasing Steps:

First row: Yarns will travel right to left in "stick-shed." Decrease left diamond yarn one warp to left. Increase right white yarn one warp to the left.

Second row: Yarns will travel left to right in "pull-shed." Left white yarn meets diamond yarn by going one warp *more.* Right diamond

yarn meets right white yarn by going one warp *less.*

MIDDLE OF THE WEAVING

When you are at the middle of your weaving, plan your attack on the next half. Plan out your design using various considerations mentioned in the *Understanding Design* section of the book. Use some of your own ideas. Be sure you have a design which will hold your interest. Completion of the project is of the essence.

SECOND HALF OF WEAVING: "The Countdown"

The second half of the weaving will continue much as before. As you progress you will notice, however, that the weaving space becomes smaller and smaller. This occurrence brings into action some of the smaller weaving tools. Timing and suggestions for the advantageous use of each are listed below.

1. *When you are 9 to 10″ from the top of your weaving,* change to your smaller batten (½″ size). Since space is at a premium, keep shed rods up out of the way of the fork as far as possible.

Persevere as the space keeps getting tighter.

Remember that Navajo rugs have been woven for centuries by this method. *It is possible!*

Use of Small Stick

As weaving space becomes uncomfortable for fingers, a small stick

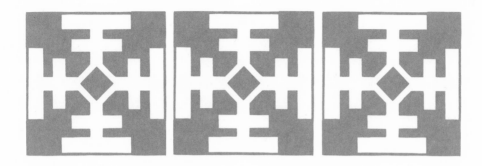

(about 6″) with a broken end may be used as a mini-shuttle. For each color separately, twirl end of yarn with broken end of stick and poke through shed.

2. *When you have 4″ to go,* change to an even smaller batten. If you do not have one, you may remove top shed dowel, refine its point and use this.

Substitute an even smaller reed for this shed rod, if possible. If you do not have a smaller reed to act as a shed rod, remove it entirely and refer to No. 3 for detailed directions on weaving technique once shed rod is removed.

Modification of Fork Technique

During this time you will notice that you can no longer tamp weft into position in regular fashion, as tines of the fork hit shed rods. Packing the weft now takes the form of *bearing down.* When pressing with the fork, facile Navajo weavers usually lead with the edge of the fork nearest the bound end of weft. After initial pressure on this side, they then rotate the tines pressing with the other edge. Moving across weaving row, this rocking motion provides ample weft in a tight spot.

3. *When you have 2″ to go* and still have a top shed rod, remove it. You now have only the heddle rod to open the shed. Utilize the "pull-shed" as before; create the opposite shed by threading small batten through opposite warp. Follow with yarn on umbrella rib or sacking needle, depending on design.

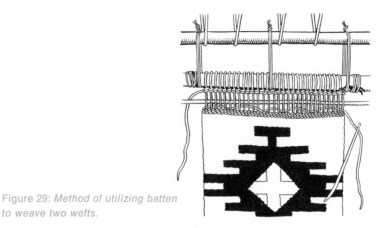

Figure 29: *Method of utilizing batten to weave two wefts.*

Use of Umbrella Rib

The umbrella rib may be used as an oversized needle. If the eye is large enough, thread weft directly. If not, thread string through, tie in loop and use this loop as a larger eye.

The umbrella rib, you will discover, is especially functional when weaving a solid stripe.

Once design is completed and final stripe is begun, a new technique may be employed to facilitate weaving:

     a. Weave in top 4 yellow rows as you did the first 4, going under and over each pair of warps. After each row, push weft up to top of weaving. Complete 4 rows in such manner.

     b. After 4 rows are completed, thread batten over and under alternate warps as in regular weave. Once batten is in position, utilize its presence to weave 2 wefts in the same shed: one row on top of batten which you push upward, and one row beneath batten which you push downward to the weaving line.

     c. When these wefts are packed in place, remove batten and re-thread it through the alternate shed, again utilizing its position for 2 wefts.

When heddle rod is of no more use, remove. (Slide rod from loops and pull string out.)

4. *Final Thrust Into the Homestretch:*

Eventually you will not be able even to insert the batten. At this point use only the sacking needle, all the while packing the weft as firmly as possible with fork. Keep weaving in wefts until you are certain that you cannot insert another. Then, directing pointed tines of fork between rows of weft, pack the last 1″ down even more firmly. This will probably open up another ¼″.

Once again insert as many wefts as possible. Again you will come to the point where you are absolutely positive you cannot insert another row. At this point *force in 4 more wefts.* Be motivated by the fact that were you a Navajo weaver selling your weaving to a Trading Post, the trader would try to tell your starting from your finishing end. Do not let the finished end be thinner. Packing should be so tight that a fingernail forced into the web cannot be felt on the reverse side. The warps should not show through from sparseness of weft. Force the remaining wefts into place and you will then be finished.

REMOVE WEAVING FROM LOOM

When you have forced in as many wefts as the warp is physically able to accommodate, you may pronounce your weaving completed and remove it from the loom.

1. Loosen and then remove top rope.
2. Untie wire around dowels.
3. Remove twine binding from the two dowels.
4. If you used side-edging cords in addition to the end ones, these should all be tied together at corners. Therefore, untie end-edging cord knots and re-tie again with the side-edging cords included.
5. If there are any problems with the finished appearance of your weaving, consult chapter on *Remedies.*

HANDLES

Your weaving is now complete. It may be used flat on the table, or hung on the wall. For those planning to fold it into a purse or bag, ideas for handles follow.

A strap should be designed in response to the purpose of the bag. If used as a purse, a handle long enough to extend along the sides gives the purse added body and style. A strap on a tool bag or medicine pouch, which is worn diagonally across the body, would need additional length. A smoke-pouch would not need any, while the knapsack may require two, one on each side to accommodate arms.

Straps may be woven or braided.

The Woven Handle

The woven handle, being the wider of the two, can be utilized to add its width to that of the purse. This would be convenient in terms of additional visibility and accessibility of contents. A book- or binder-carrier would likewise benefit from the wider width.

A strap can be woven on an inkle loom, if you have one, or with a rigid heddle. A good width is 1½". When sewing the handle to the bag, attach end to middle of weaving and then stitch the sides of the weaving up along the sides of the handle. Use a flat running stitch: with the weft thread and sacking needle, alternately pick up a few weft edges from the weaving, and then a few from the strap. Continue along sides until joining is complete.

The Braided Handle

The braided handle is a much quicker solution and has a roundness which feels good to the hand. In addition, it requires no loom or special equipment to make.

When attaching the braided handle to the purse, sew the sides together first and then attach the handle over this seam.

Fasteners

A variety of fasteners may be used to close the bag. The simplest is a loop on the back side which connects with a button on the front. Another possibility is to install a cotton lining in which a zipper has been sewn. Side pockets can also be incorporated in this manner. Metal strips, which pull apart to open and snap together to close, may also be used. The success of this method depends on the length of the metal strips coinciding with the width of the purse. The chapter on *Supply Sources* contains size and source details.

EMBELLISHMENTS

You may find it fun to personalize your bag. Add your own kind of trim. Use the weaving as a base and let your imagination go!

Let fringe swing from the ends of the handles. Knot it through the

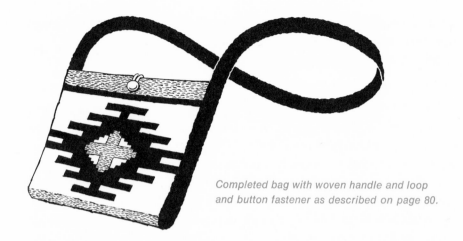

Completed bag with woven handle and loop and button fastener as described on page 80.

middle of the weaving to sway clear across the bottom of the completed bag.

Use buttons — old Navajo tarnished silver buttons, organic buttons, any to suit your taste. Sew them around the opening of the bag, incorporate them into the design, attach them at intervals along the handle — all reminiscent of the old Navajo medicine man pouches.

Coordinate your Navajo weaving with macrame. Macrame the fringe; macrame the handle. Use a heavy-knotted feeling so the unity of the two techniques will be more apparent than the contrast.

THINK FORWARD

You may think of this time as one of completion, or you may consider it a time of innovation and beginning. In either case, remember the wisdom of the loom: *A weaver has four days in which to begin her next weaving.*

Rewarp the loom, spin yarn, collect dye plants, plan the design. For four days after your weaving is completed, think forward toward the next . . . so that there may be continuity between weavings.

And may the next weaving be even better than the last!

Loom Problems

LOP-SIDED WARP (remedy used with wool warp)

If at anytime you discover the tension of the warp is unequal, begin at left and gently pull each top warp until the tension is equalized. If tension corrects itself, continue on to next step. If it does not, remove and redo with greater concentration and precision. Placing the warp frame on table throughout warping frequently helps. Although not traditionally Navajo, this system has proven effective.

Tool Problems

DIFFICULTY IN INSERTING BATTEN

Reread section on batten insertion (page 43). If remedy is not clear, consider the following:

1. If fibers on warps are sticking together, strum warp with back of fingers preliminary to batten insertion.

2. If forward curved end of batten continually goes behind back warps instead of in shed, the curve of the batten may not be sufficient.

Try inserting batten by holding it vertically, parallel to warp. Drop top end into shed.

3. If batten hits vertical post upon insertion, check horizontals on loom to be certain they cross in front of the vertical loom supports, thereby holding weaving in front of loom proper. Batten can also be inserted by the above method in No. 2 to avoid vertical posts.

SLIPPERY FORK

Occasionally an extended period of weaving causes the fork to become slippery and fall from your hand. In such instances the possibility of the tines cracking is of concern. Slipperiness can be remedied by application of adhesive tape or yarn about the handle.

Weaving Problems

SELVAGE EDGES GOING IN (the most common of weaving difficulties)

Causes:
   1. Warp needs tightening.
   2. Weft needs to be laid in more loosely.

Remedies:
   1. Measure width of weaving frequently as a preventative action. Unravel a few rows when uneven edge is first spotted.
   2. Tighten warp if needed; a tight warp will not move easily.
   3. Watch weft as it circles edge; edge warps should not be pulled in.
   4. Watch joints of colors: At a color-joint the tension should be tight. As a color travels over its own design, the weft should be loose.
   5. Check to see if warp threads are becoming too close in one section. If so, see remedy for this.
   6. If in a large design area, the edges are going in, lay weft in loosely via scallops.
   7. Tie side of weaving snugly to vertical posts about 1″ below weaving level. This will pull and retain edge out to proper width.
   8. Some weavers loop a string between the vertical post and the free side warps. The string can be slid up out of the way while weaving, or down to provide an instant gauge.

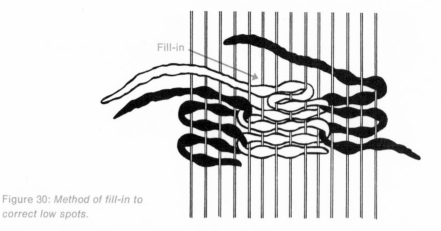

Fill-in

Figure 30: *Method of fill-in to correct low spots.*

SELVAGE EDGES GOING OUT

Causes:

1. Warp too loose.
2. Weft too loose in shed.
3. Weft too big for the size of spaces between the warp.

Remedies:

1. Tighten warp.
2. Reduce size of scallops so weft will not be as generous.
3. Unspin yarn and pull out to create a finer weft. Respin.

LOW SPOTS

Causes:

1. One color of yarn finer than rest.
2. One color of yarn with looser twist than rest even though diameter is the same as the others.
3. Uneven spinning, such that for a period of time one color has above characteristics.

Remedies:

1. This phenomenon should be corrected upon first notice. If left alone, the problem is usually intensified and therefore demands increasingly more attention.
2. As soon as low spot is recognized, fill in as in figure 30.

The "fill-in" becomes imperceptible upon being packed in place.

WARPS TOO CLOSE IN ONE SECTION

In the course of weaving you may notice that the warps have eased together in one section. The following are indications of this:

1. Edges are going in.

2. Weft won't pack down. (Weft does not have room to go around each warp comfortably and settle into place.)

3. High spot: Because of insufficient room to settle, wefts stack.

Causes:

This sometimes occurs where weft is being laid in too tight or in sections where weft is thinner and does not hold warps apart.

Remedies:

1. Tighten warp.

2. Use pointed end of fork for following procedure: In section of close warps, lift successive weft up for 1″ beneath weaving line. Move warps individually toward section with the biggest spaces. Beat down again.

3. Alternate method: The above is the gentle version of the Navajo remedy. Adroit Navajo weavers poke end of fork between warps for about 1″ below the weaving level, to force wefts upward and warps apart. The point is then mercilessly dragged from center of tight section outward in both directions to distribute warps.

Unfortunately, warps do not move much unless this motion is done mercilessly. This is indeed unfortunate since this procedure, clumsily done, frequently causes a weak thread to snap. Be prepared to turn to section on warp repair, if you choose the alternate method.

4. After warps are separated and weft is once again in position, carefully lay in ample weft at this section to keep warps apart.

RIDGES AT JOINTS

There is always some unevenness of texture at joints of colors. However, if heavy ridges are occurring, try pulling weft tight at the actual joint, and then laying it loosely thereafter.

RIPPLING MATERIAL

Rippling material is the result of uneven weft tension. Whereas looseness usually occurs where there is little or no pattern, tightness coincides with more complex pattern and joints.

1. The best remedy is constant measurement to determine when the edge begins to go in or out. At this point a few rows may be taken out and rewoven for a permanent correction. And although unraveling is never pleasant, one can be motivated by considering that the amount of time spent unraveling is insignificant compared to the amount of time you will spend living with the weaving and wishing you had taken the time to correct it.

2. See sections on *Edges Going In, Edges Going out,* and *Difficulty with Material Upon Completion,* for additional corrections.

HOW TO REPAIR BROKEN WARP

The method of repairing a broken warp is dependent in many respects on where the break occurs.

How to repair when break is well *above the weaving line.*

1. Tie new piece of warp to the two broken ends.
2. Use square knots.
3. Be sure tension on repaired warp is comparable to other warps.

How to repair when break is *at weaving line.*

1. Run sacking needle with new warp along broken warp strand.

Start about 2″ below the weaving line and work your way amid the wefts so the new and old warps are together.

2. Tie upper end of new warp to top of broken warp (square knot). Trim ends from about 1″ from knot.

3. Direct lower end of new warp out rear of fabric. Tie to lower beam of loom. Upon completion of project excess warp is trimmed.

Problems Upon Completion

CORNERS TURN UP

1. Weft may not be packed tightly enough.

2. If you have used a side selvage cord, this may be too tight. If this is the case, simply loosen and retie.

SURFACE RIPPLES

This is caused by unequal tension of weft during weaving. If there is an area which ripples the full width of the weaving, this can be lessened through steam pressing.

1. Wet clean cloth.

2. Place upon area you wish to press, and apply iron.

Do not place hot iron directly on weaving. This spoils the texture as well as introducing the possibility of scorching.

Navajo Warp and Weft see chapter on *Yarns*

Other Warp and Weft see chapter on *Yarns*

Since prices may fluctuate, none have been included here. We suggest that you contact the supply sources and request catalogs or price lists.

Navajo Looms

LIVING DESIGNS: Dedicated to Navajo weaving exclusively.
Looms made according to specifications in book.
Highly stable construction, 3′ x 4′ size.
Willow sticks, 1″ dowels, and ⅜″ cotton rope included.
Custom sizes and woods available.
Send for brochure.

SOME PLACE:
Redwood with oil finish.
3′ widths in 4′ and 5′ heights.
Send for brochure.

Forks and Battens

LIVING DESIGNS: Dedicated to Navajo weaving exclusively.

All tools are *hand-hewn by Navajo toolmakers* from reservation hardwoods such as cedar, oak, wild holly, and mahogany root.

Forks in two sizes:

All-purpose size (approximately 1½″) for weaving and finishing — adequate for small project in book. Large size (over 1½″) for glorious weaving and heavy packing.

Battens with essential curve:

Three sizes: small (under ¾″), medium (¾″ - 1½″), and large (over 1½″).

Spindles also available; send for brochure.

NAVAJO TRAILS SHOPPING CENTER   89

CUSTOM HANDWEAVERS:

The above sources offer *Navajo-made forks and curved battens* in a variety of sizes and woods.

BRUCE GILLAN:

Forks and battens in a wide variety of hardwoods.

Production unpredictable. Send for brochure. Order direct or through CASA DE LAS TEJEDORAS.

SOME PLACE:

Forks 2″ x 12″ in hardwood. Light and heavy weights.

Battens with bent tip. Hardwood, ½″, 1″, 1½″.

Spindles also available; send for brochure.

Sacking Needles

LIVING DESIGNS:

Expanded point and large eye 5″ needle. The equivalent sold at SOME PLACE and NAVAJO TRAILS.

Handbag Fasteners

CRAFT SERVICE:

"Facile" Handbag Fastener.

Available sizes: 7″ - 8″ - 9″ - 10″ - 11″ - 12″.

Addresses of Supply Sources

CASA DE LAS TEJEDORAS
1619 East Edinger
Santa Ana, California 92705

CRAFT SERVICE
337–341 University Avenue
Rochester, New York 14607

CUSTOM HANDWEAVERS
Allied Arts Guild
Arbor Road at Creek Drive
Menlo Park, California 94025

90

DHARMA TRADING CO.
Mailing Address: Box 1288
Location: 1952 University Avenue
Berkeley, California 94701

GILLAN, BRUCE
Mailing Address: Box 633
Solana Beach, California 92075

HANDCRAFT HOUSE
110 West Esplanade
North Vancouver, B.C., Canada

KNIT AND PURL YARN SHOP
2158½ N. 4th St.
Flagstaff, Arizona 86001

LILY MILLS CO.
Handweaving Department
Shelby, North Carolina 28150

LIVING DESIGNS
7535 Sunset Way
Aptos, California 95003

NAVAJO TRAILS SHOPPING
   CENTER
P. O. Box 37
Tuba City, Arizona 86045

THE PENDLETON SHOP
Box 233, Jordan Road
Sedona, Arizona 86336

SOME PLACE
2990 Adeline St.
Berkeley, California 94703

THE YARN DEPOT
545 Sutter Street *closed*
San Francisco, California 94102

Appendix

Information on techniques which are beyond the scope of the described project

I. Modifications for Looms Whose Stability is Inadequate

1. Legs: Replace or add legs 2″ x 4″ x 30″, placed at bottom outer edges of frame. Bolt, screw or nail into position. (See section on *Loom Construction* for details.)

2. Back and front crosspieces: Nail 2 x 4's between the legs at the back and the front of the loom to provide weight. Bricks may be placed on top of back crosspiece if it is determined that additional weight is needed.

3. Top beam: Attach a 1″ pipe or dowel which is longer than the width of the loom, to create a top beam which will hold the weaving in front of the loom proper. (See directions for securing this beam under section on *Loom Construction.*)

4. Bottom beam: Attach pipe (or dowel) at bottom of loom. Let it rest on the 2″ x 4″ legs and attach with 2 pipe straps screwed into position. (See section on *Loom Construction* for details.)

5. Dowels: The 3 dowels that come with the loom should be longer than width of loom. If they are not, replace accordingly.

II. Warp Spinning and Treatment

1. If you spin your own warp or buy warp which requires additional spinning, use the following treatment to set spin and remove kinks:

   a. On spinning wheel or spindle create a fine, tightly-spun, strong warp which is resistant to abrasion. Spinning between palms is time consuming but possible.

    b. Dip hand in water and trail it over a portion of the warp. Wind this moist warp *tightly* into a ball. Continue until entire warp is moistened and wound. A thread spool or rock is a convenient item to use as a foundation for the ball. Let dry several days; the warp is ready for use when dry.

If respun warp is not given the above treatment, the curly overtwisted yarn is difficult to work with and often snaps during the warping process.

III. Side Selvage Cords

The traditional purpose of side selvage cords is to provide added durability to heavy-duty items which get excessive wear on edges (saddle blankets, floor rugs, etc.). However, some Anglo weavers use them for sheer aesthetics.

The method here initially describes twining a double cord. A tripled cord is also possible and increases both wearability and aesthetics. Directions for both follow.

There are a variety of ways to incorporate side selvage cords. The one presented here provides for greatest wearability and least difficulty in retaining straight edges. With this method, one strand of each doubled selvage cord is included right along with the edge warp for about 6 turns of the weft (12 rows). The strands are then twisted and the free strand substituted for the next 6 weft turns.

When methods are used in which the cord is not bound with the edge warp, but instead forms its own warp, the precision of tension required by this cord can cause difficulties. The cord must be tight enough to keep the edge straight, but loose enough so that the project upon completion and removal will not pucker, ripple or curl.

MATERIALS NEEDED

Two lengths of 2-ply cord (see section on *Yarn* for directions). Each should be four times the length of the weaving plus 20″. (Increase by more than 20″ for large projects.)

INSTALLATION PROCEDURE

After loom is strung up and shed rods positioned:

    1. Double a two-ply cord. Secure looped end to bottom dowel along left side of warp. The fastening should wrap over the binding and use about 5″ of cord. These ends will ultimately tie with ends of edging cord upon completion of project.

    2. Pass cord behind shed rods and then to the top dowel, at left of warp. Wrap twice around dowel and slip end through the wrapping. Tension is snug but not as tight as warp.

    3. Repeat on right side with second two-ply cord.

USING SELVAGE CORDS ON 10″ x 23″ PROJECT

Place one strand of each doubled selvage cord in front of top shed rod. The strands in front of the shed rod will be woven with the edge warps as follows:

    Row 1: Set-up: Loom strung with even number of warps. Weft to be woven right to left.

    As you insert batten in "stick-shed" pick up forward selvage strand on the left side.

    Lay in weft from right to left. (On left edge, weft will pass between selvage strands.)

    Row 2: Set-up: Weft at left of weaving. Before batten goes into "pull-shed," pick up forward strand of selvage cord on right side. Continue batten on through shed, ignoring both selvage strands on left, and thus leaving both behind batten.

    Lay in weft, left to right. (Weft will turn around the forward selvage strand on left side, and go between the two strands on right side.)

    Row 3: Same as No. 1.

    Row 4: Same as No. 2.

    Continue to Row No. 12 where a strand of each edging cord will have 6 weft turns on it.

Two Rules:

When loom is strung with even number of warps:

    When inserting batten pick up forward selvage strand on side where edge warp crosses in front of batten.

When loom is strung with odd number of warps:

When both edge warps are in front position, include front strand of each selvage cord on front of batten.

In following row both cords remain behind.

THE TWIST

Remove the bound selvage strand from in front of shed rod. Replace it with the free one as follows:

On each side separately:

1. Reach between bound selvage strand and edge warp.
2. Grasp free edging strand and pull through.
3. Place in front of top shed rod to hold it forward. Continue weaving for 12 more rows, binding this new strand to the edge warp as before. After 12 rows (6 weft turns) the strands are exchanged in like manner.

Throughout the alternation there will always be 2 threads bound together by the weft (one edge warp and one of the selvage strands). There will always be one selvage strand left outside to provide a visible and functional edging.

A continually increasing twist will develop above the shed rod. After a while it will be necessary to untie top of selvage cords, untwist and retie as before.

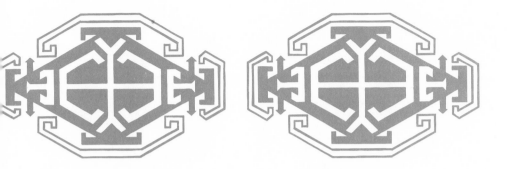

TRIPLE SELVAGE CORD

A more decorative three-strand cord may also be used in the same way. Initially tie three cords instead of two along each edge. Alternate the binding of these three in succession. This will leave two cords outside for a stronger, more ornate edge.

IV. When Length of Weaving Exceeds Height of Loom

MOUNTING INSTRUCTIONS

1. Connect dowel No. 1 to lower beam (pipe) as in mounting instructions. Also connect dowel No. 2 to dowel No. 3.

2. Lay strung warp over top beam of loom so dowel No. 3 hangs in back of the weaving.

3. Secure additional beam to rear of loom about one foot below dowel No. 3.

4. Rope dowel No. 3 to new beam via mounting directions.

5. As you are weaving and the height gets too high to continue comfortably, follow directions for "Rolling Weaving Under Bottom Beam" (next section).

V. Rolling Weaving Under Bottom Beam

The Navajo weaver sitting on the floor of her hogan regulates the weaving level so it is always within reach. If weaving is within the

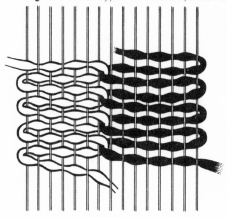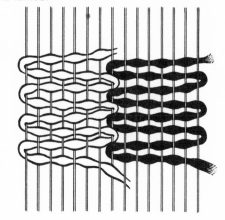

96

size of the loom, successively higher seats may be used to raise the weaver as the weaving itself grows. If the weaving is longer than the loom, or if the weaver wishes to remain in floor position, the weaving may be lowered as follows:

    1. If top of warp is behind loom as described in IV. above, untie rope. If top of warp is in front of loom, loosen rope and proceed.

    2. Untie bottom dowel from bottom pipe (beam).

    3. Direct bottom dowel (No. 1) beneath pipe and up back of loom. Secure dowel here so weaving goes down beneath pipe and up front of loom. Weaving level should be about 7″ above pipe.

    4. Refasten rope to top beam and tighten.

VARIOUS TECHNIQUES FOR SECURING DOWEL

    1. Secure with drilled hole and lashing method, as described for the top beam.

    2. Secure with pipe strap.

    3. Secure by hammering nail in front of vertical posts of loom, slightly above where dowel will be secured in rear. Tie dowel to post, hooking rope over nail to resist downward pull.

VI. Vertical Joining

There are basically two kinds of vertical joints, "hooked" and "turned."

    1. The "hooked" joint is the one most commonly used in Navajo

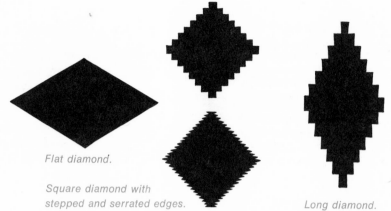

Flat diamond.

Square diamond with
stepped and serrated edges.

Long diamond.

97

weaving due to its strength. Its other asset, the fact that the joints occur between warps, is responsible for nominal buildup when used for a prolonged vertical, such as in a border. Ridges are its main setback.

2. The "turned" joint is used alternatively. Some strength is sacrificed and as a result, there are some weavers who refuse to use it in a rug. Buildup, due to the occurrence of 4 wefts and a warp at the joint instead of the usual 2, can cause problems with prolonged use.

VII. Diagonal Joining

There are many variations on weaving the diagonal pattern. The technique you select is determined by aesthetics and by physical properties. The shape of the diamond (thus the inclination of the diagonal slope) as well as the kind of edge you want, are the aesthetic considerations. The physical considerations include the size of the weft you are using, the distance between your warps, and the strength required of the joint.

The three main shapes possible are:

1. The Flat Diamond

   This is the easiest and gives the smoothest edge.
2. The Square Diamond

   This one has a choice of edges: stepped or serrated.
3. The Long Diamond

   This design is usually stepped.

98

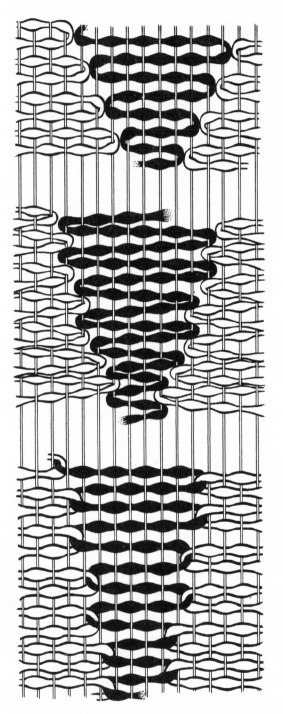

Detail of flat diamond technique (smooth edge).

Detail of serrated diamond technique.

Detail of stepped diamond technique.

120 Warps 24

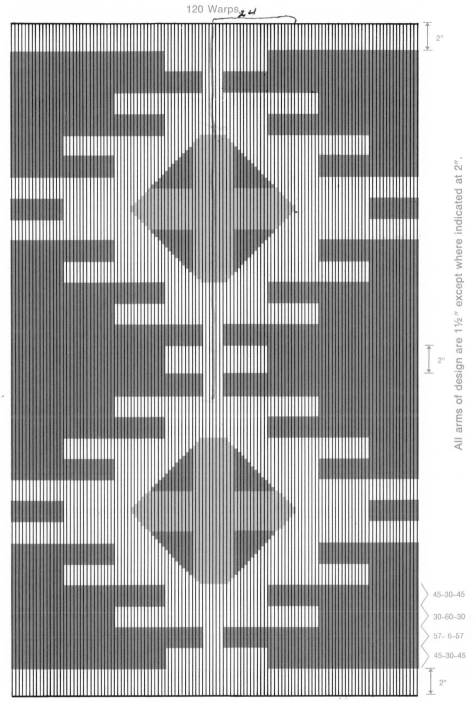

2"

All arms of design are 1½" except where indicated at 2".

99

2"

45–30–45
30–60–30
57– 6–57
45–30–45

2"

DIAGRAM FOR LARGER RUG: Size: 2½' x 4' • Warp Spacing: 121 marks on dowel #1, 120 marks on dowel #2 • Approximate Warp Required: 250 yards • Approximate Weft Required: 3½ lbs. — brown 2 lbs. • white 1 lb. • orange ½ lb.

Glossary of Terms

BATTEN: A flattened, smoothed wooden tool used to keep the shed open while a weft is inserted.

EDGING AND SELVAGE CORD: Two-ply handspun yarn used on edges of weaving in selvage position. For distinguishing purposes, "edging cord" refers to the binding at the top and bottom, while "selvage cord" pertains to those on the sides.

HEDDLE ROD: A device for reversing the warp position described above. A stick is placed horizontally in front of the warps and string is looped from the rod to those warps in back position. When the heddle rod is pulled, these back warps come forward to create the "pull-shed."

HOOKED JOINT: A method of joining two colors by hooking that results in no loss of strength in the final woven product.

LAY-IN (of a yarn): A method of introducing a new yarn into the weft by trailing the tapered end through the shed until it is just inside the new design area.

OVERLAPPING JOINT: A method of piecing yarn by overlapping the tapered ends.

PULL-SHED: An opening between front and back warps created by separating the two shed rods, and pulling on the heddle rod. In this manner the back warps are brought into a forward position. A batten is inserted and a weft may be passed.

SCALLOPS or BUBBLING: A means of laying weft loosely into a shed so as to control weft tension.

SHED: The opening between front and back warps through which a weft is passed. The shed is created by manipulation of rods and held open by the batten turned on edge.

SHED ROD: A stick passed behind alternate warps for the purpose of holding every other warp forward, and creating the opening into which a batten may be inserted for the "stick-shed."

SQUARE KNOT: The basic knot used in Navajo weaving, made with two ends as follows:
       Left over right, around and through.
       Right over left, around and through.

STICK-SHED: An opening between front and back warps created by positioning the shed and heddle rods together. A batten, inserted below the rods, holds the warps apart for passage of a weft.

STICK-SHUTTLE: A dry straight twig on which weft is wrapped, and by means of which weft is carried through the shed from side to side in areas of solid stripe.

TAPESTRY WEAVE: The most common Navajo weave in which wefts are beaten so closely together as to completely cover the warp.

TWO-PLY YARN: Two single strands of yarn which are twisted together and function as edging cords in Navajo weaving.

WARP: The yarn initially stretched on the loom in preparation for the actual weaving.

WARP TURN OR WARP PAIR: A phenomenon originating during the warping process when a warp is carried over a dowel and returned back toward the weaver, thus creating a warp turn, or pair of warps. These two warps are treated as a unit during the edging process, during the binding, and again in the first and final four rows of the weaving.

WEAVING LINE: The horizontal line across which the weft is moving, or: Where the action's at!

WEFT: The yarn that is woven over and under the warp and from side to side.

Suggested Readings

Amsden, Charles A. *Navajo Weaving, Its Technique and History.* Santa Ana, California: Rio Grande Press. First published 1934, reprinted 1964.

Bartlett, Katharine. "Present Trends in Weaving on the Western Navajo Reservation." Flagstaff: *Plateau,* Museum of Northern Arizona, July 1966, pp. 1–6.

Bennett, Noël. *The Weaver's Pathway: A Clarification of the "Spirit Trail" in Navajo Weaving.* Flagstaff: Northland Press, 1974.

Bryan, Nonabah G. and Young, Stella. *Navajo Native Dyes, Their Preparation and Use.* U. S. Department of Interior, Bureau of Indian Affairs, Indian Handcraft Series No. 2. Education Division, 1940.

Dutton, Bertha P. *Navajo Weaving Today.* Santa Fe: Museum of New Mexico Press, 1961.

James, George Wharton. *Indian Blankets and Their Makers.* New York: Tudor Publishing Co., 1937. Originally published 1914, A. C. McClurg and Co., Boston.

Kent, Kate Peck. *The Story of Navajo Weaving.* Phoenix: Heard Museum of Anthropology and Primitive Art, 1962.

Matthews, George Washington. *Navajo Weavers.* 3rd Annual Report of the Bureau of Ethnology, 1884. Reprint, Filter Press, 1968.

Maxwell, Gilbert S. *Navajo Rugs — Past, Present, and Future.* Palm Desert, California: Desert-Southwest, Inc., 1963.

Pendleton, Mary. "Navajo Weaving." *The Looming Arts,* 4:4,5,6 (1969); 5:1,2,3,4,5,6 (1970). Some succeeding issues.

Reichard, Gladys A. *Navajo Shepherd and Weaver.* Locust Valley, New York: J. J. Augustin, 1936. Reprinted Santa Fe: Rio Grande Press, 1968.

——. *Spider Woman, A Story of Navajo Weavers and Chanters.* New York: Macmillan, 1934. Reprinted Santa Fe: Rio Grande Press, 1968.

105